7 The HABITS of HIGHLY EFFECTIVE PEOPLE
PERSONAL WORKBOOK

STEPHEN R. COVEY

SIMON &
SCHUSTER

London   New York   Sydney   Toronto

First published in Great Britain by Simon & Schuster UK Ltd, 2005
A CBS COMPANY

Designed by Katy Riegel

13

Simon & Schuster UK Ltd
1st Floor
222 Gray's Inn Road
London WC1X 8HB

www.simonandschuster.co.uk

Simon & Schuster Australia
Sydney

A CIP catalogue record for this book is available from the British Library

ISBN 10: 0-7432-6816-4
ISBN 13: 978-0-7432-6816-5

Printed and bound in the UK by
CPI Group (UK) Ltd, Croydon, CR0 4YY

CONTENTS

ABOUT THIS
PERSONAL WORKBOOK

IN THESE CHALLENGING TIMES, we see rapid change all around us. Some changes are for the better, compelling us to alter or adapt the way we think or the way we live. But other changes may leave us feeling unsettled, confused, and ineffective. The *7 Habits of Highly Effective People* provides an anchor for our lives—enabling us to live with a sense of constancy amid change—because the habits are based on timeless, universal, self-evident principles of human effectiveness.

This companion workbook to *The 7 Habits of Highly Effective People* will provide you with application exercises as well as the opportunity to make notes, record your thoughts, score yourself on self-assessments, and answer questions designed to provoke thought and encourage deeper insights into the reading material. At the beginning of each section you will be asked to read or reread specific chapters in *The 7 Habits of Highly Effective People. The 7 Habits of Highly Effective People* and *The 7 Habits of Highly Effective People Personal Workbook* are designed to be companions. Use them and reuse them!

If you are willing to pay the price to truly understand and apply the habits and principles taught in the book and this workbook, you will reap powerful benefits. You will find your time and activities increasingly becoming a matter of your *choices,* and that you can truly live a richer, happier, and more fulfilling life. You will notice an acceleration of personal development and improvement, and will also discover increased emotional strength and greater self-discipline. You will see an increase in the quality and effectiveness of your relationships on every level.

We hope your experience with this workbook will be both empowering and enjoyable as you learn and relearn these timeless principles of effectiveness. Give yourself the opportunity to really dig into the material presented in this workbook. Be honest with yourself and with others as you share your insights and the things you've learned. Make this material work for you!

PART ONE

PARADIGMS AND PRINCIPLES

Before you begin this section of *The 7 Habits of Highly Effective People Personal Workbook*,
read pages 15–62 in *The 7 Habits of Highly Effective People*.

PARADIGMS

*Our paradigms, correct or incorrect, are the sources of our attitudes
and behaviors, and ultimately our relationships with others.*
—STEPHEN R. COVEY

A STORE MANAGER HEARD one of his salespeople say to a customer,
"No, we haven't had any for some weeks now, and it doesn't look as if we'll be
getting any soon." The manager was shocked to hear these words and rushed
to the customer as she was walking out. "That isn't true," he said, but she just
gave him an odd look and walked out. He confronted the salesperson and
said, "Never, never say we don't have something. If we don't have it, say we've
ordered it and it's on its way. Now, what did she want?"

"Rain," said the salesperson.

How many times have you made assumptions similar to the store manager's? It's easy to do, because we all see things in different ways. We all have
different paradigms or frames of reference—like eyeglasses through which we
see the world. We see the world not as it is, but as we are—or sometimes as we
are conditioned to see it.

The more we are aware of our basic paradigms, or assumptions, and the
extent to which we have been influenced by our experiences, the more we
can take responsibility for those paradigms, examine them, test them against
reality, change them if necessary, and listen to others and be open to their
perceptions.

It becomes obvious that if we want to make relatively minor changes in
our lives, we can focus on our attitudes and behaviors. But if we want to make
significant quantum changes, we need to work on our basic paradigms—the
way we view ourselves and the world around us.

Have you ever had an experience where you made an assumption, only to find that you had jumped to a conclusion too quickly? Describe the experience below.

_____

_____

_____

_____

_____

What was the assumption you made?

_____

_____

_____

_____

_____

Think about some other assumptions you may have made. What will you do this week to work on one of them?

_____

_____

_____

_____

EXAMINING YOUR PARADIGMS

Have you ever been to a different country or even to a different region in your country? What was strange to you?

_____

_____

_____

_____

_____

Did people act the way you expected them to? What did you think about their actions?

_____

_____

_____

_____

Looking back on your travel experiences now, what do you think people thought about you? Do you believe their thoughts about you were probably similar to your thoughts about them?

_____

_____

_____

_____

If you had the opportunity to get to know people in your travels, how did that change your assumptions about them?

_____

_____

_____

_____

_____

SHIFTING YOUR PARADIGM

Think about the different routes you can take to your home or work. Are some ways more complex than others? Is one way sometimes more convenient than another? Why or why not?

_____

_____

_____

_____

_____

Have you ever found a new way home that you didn't know existed? What were the unexpected feelings of traveling different routes?

_____

_____

_____

_____

_____

Now think about the way you interact with people. Are there several ways to approach them? What new ways might you try?

_____

_____

_____

_____

_____

PRINCIPLES

It is impossible for us to break the law. We can only break ourselves against the law.
                                                    —CECIL B. DEMILLE

ONCE EINSTEIN SAW the needle of a compass at the age of four, he always understood that there had to be "something behind things, something deeply hidden." This also pertains to every other realm of life. Principles are *universal*—that is, they transcend culture and geography. They're also *timeless,* they never change—principles such as fairness, kindness, respect, honesty, integrity, service, contribution. Different cultures may translate these principles into different practices and over time may even totally obscure these principles through the wrongful use of freedom. Nevertheless, they are present. Like the law of gravity, they operate constantly.

Principles are also *inarguable.* That is, they are self-evident. For example, you can never have enduring trust without trustworthiness. Think about it; that is a natural law.

Natural laws (like gravity) and principles (like respect, honesty, kindness, integrity, and fairness) control the consequences of our choices. Just as you get bad air and bad water when you consistently violate the environment, so also is trust (the glue of relationships) destroyed when you're consistently unkind and dishonest to people.

Remember Aesop's fable "The Goose and the Golden Egg"? The moral of this fable has a modern application. True effectiveness is a function of two things: that which is produced (the golden eggs), and the producing asset or capacity to produce (the goose). Like the foolish farmer, we often emphasize short-term results at the expense of long-term prosperity.

Effectiveness lies in the balance: the P/PC Balance®. "P" stands for production of desired results—the golden eggs. "PC" stands for production capability—the ability or asset that produces the golden egg.

In spite of the obvious need for balancing P and PC, we frequently neglect and abuse physical, financial, and human resources. For instance, we don't properly maintain our bodies, the environment, or our valuable physical possessions. Of equal concern, we overlook relationships, neglecting kindnesses and courtesies.

On the other hand, PC investments such as exercising and eating properly, increasing skills, and developing relationships contribute to our quality of life. Relationships are stronger, finances are more secure, and physical assets last longer.

Reflect on Aesop's fable "The Goose and the Golden Egg." Take a few moments and write your own fable about yourself. In terms of your production and production capability, where do you need to develop greater balance? Here's an example to help get you thinking:

A talented and enterprising young woman was a wife, mother, and businesswoman. She wanted to do a good job for herself, her family, and her company. She worked hard and was soon recognized as someone whom people could depend on to get things done quickly, efficiently, and with high quality, whether at home or at work. Things began piling up. She came home barely in time to put the kids to bed. The quality of her life diminished on every level. She felt tired all the time, and she ended up feeling used and abused.

_____

_____

_____

_____

_____

_____

_____

...ts center on timeless and universal principles of personal, inter-
..., managerial, and organizational effectiveness. Listed here are the
...ples upon which the Habits are based.

1. The principle of continuous learning, of self-reeducation—the discipline that drives us toward the values we believe in. Such constant learning
is required in today's world. Continuous learning is part of what keeps us feeling empowered in our relationships and accomplished in our work. Technol-
ogy is constantly changing, and many of us will work in more than five
different fields before we retire. Are you willing to be left behind?

*That is what learning is. You suddenly understand something you've under-
stood all your life, but in a new way.* —DORIS LESSING

2. The principle of service, of giving oneself to others, of helping to facili-
tate other people in their endeavors.

*To serve is beautiful, but only if it is done with joy and a whole heart and a
free mind.* —PEARL S. BUCK

3. The principle of staying positive and optimistic, radiating positive energy, and avoiding the four emotional cancers (criticizing, complaining, com-
paring, and competing).

*The point of living, and of being an optimist, is to be foolish enough to be-
lieve the best is yet to come.* —PETER USTINOV

4. The principle of affirmation of others—treating people as proactive
individuals who have great potential.

*Treat people as if they were what they should be, and you help them become
what they are capable of becoming.* —JOHANN WOLFGANG VON GOETHE

5. The principle of balance—the ability to identify our various roles and
to spend appropriate amounts of time in, and focus on, all of the important
roles and dimensions of our lives. Success in one area of our life cannot compensate for neglect or failure in other areas of our life.

*Everyone is a house with four rooms: physical, mental, emotional, spiritual.
Unless we go into every room every day, even if only to keep it aired, we are
not a complete person.* —RUMER GODDEN

6. The principle of spontaneity and serendipity—the ability to experience life with a sense of adventure, excitement, and fresh rediscovery instead of trying to find a serious side to things that have no serious side.

The essence of pleasure is spontaneity. —GERMAINE GREER

7. The principle of consistent self-renewal and self-improvement in the four dimensions of one's life: physical, spiritual, mental, and social/emotional.

This is the single most powerful investment we can ever make in life—investment in ourselves, in the only instrument we have with which to deal with life and to contribute. —STEPHEN R. COVEY

List five principles that affect your life on a daily basis. In what ways are you affected? Do they impact you in positive or negative ways?

1. _____

_____

_____

_____

_____

2. _____

_____

_____

_____

3. _____

_____

_____

_____

_____

4. _____

_____

_____

_____

_____

5. _____

_____

_____

_____

_____

THE 7 HABITS—AN OVERVIEW

THE 7 HABITS ARE HABITS of effectiveness. True effectiveness is based on timeless principles that are in harmony with natural law. Effective people are guided by their own missions and manage their lives according to principles. Ineffective people follow other people's agendas and manage their lives around pressing matters.

One of the best ways to understand the 7 Habits of Highly Effective People is to study their opposites. The following chart contrasts the 7 Habits of Highly *Effective* People with the 7 Habits of Highly *Ineffective* People.

EFFECTIVE PEOPLE	INEFFECTIVE PEOPLE
HABIT 1	
Habit 1: Be Proactive®. Proactive people do more than take initiative. They recognize they are responsible for their own choices and have the freedom to choose based on principles and values rather than on moods or conditions. Proactive people are agents of change.	**Be Reactive.** Reactive people don't take responsibility for their own lives. They feel victimized—a product of circumstances, their past, and other people. They do not see themselves as the creative force of their lives.
HABIT 2	
Habit 2: Begin with the End in Mind®. Individuals, families, teams, and organizations shape their own future by creating mental vision and purpose for any project, large or small, personal or interpersonal. They identify and commit themselves to the principles, relationships, and purposes that matter most to them.	**Begin with No End in Mind.** These people lack personal vision and have not developed a deep sense of personal meaning and purpose. They have not paid the price to develop a mission statement, and they live life based on society's values instead of self-chosen values.

continued

EFFECTIVE PEOPLE (continued)	INEFFECTIVE PEOPLE (continued)
HABIT 3	
Habit 3: Put First Things First®. People who put first things first organize and execute around their most important priorities. Whatever the circumstance, they live and are driven by the principles they value most.	**Put Second Things First.** These people are crisis managers who are unable to stay focused on high-leverage tasks because of their preoccupation with circumstances, their past, or other people. They are caught up in the "thick of thin things" and are driven by urgent matters.
HABIT 4	
Habit 4: Think Win-Win®. People who think win-win have a frame of mind and heart that seeks mutual benefit and mutual respect in all interactions. They think in terms of abundance and opportunity—in terms of "we" not "me." They continually seek to build more trusting relationships with others by making deposits into the Emotional Bank Account.	**Think Win-Lose or Lose-Win.** These people have a Scarcity Mentality and see life as a zero-sum game. They have ineffective communication skills and make withdrawals from other people's Emotional Bank Accounts, resulting in a defensive mentality and adversarial feelings.
HABIT 5	
Habit 5: Seek First to Understand, Then to Be Understood®. When we listen with the intent to understand others, rather than with the intent to reply, we begin true communication and relationship building. Opportunities to then speak openly and to be understood come much more naturally and easily. Seeking to understand takes consideration; seeking to be understood takes courage. Effectiveness lies in balancing or blending the two.	**Seek First to Be Understood.** These people state first their points of view, which are based solely on their autobiography and motives, without attempting to understand others first. They blindly prescribe without first diagnosing the problem.
HABIT 6	
Habit 6: Synergize®. Synergistic people seek the third alternative with others—not my way, not your way, but a third way that is better than either of us would come up with individually. Synergy is the fruit of respecting, valuing, and even celebrating one another's differences. It's about solving problems, seizing opportunities, and working out differences. It's the kind of creative cooperation of 1 + 1 = 3, 11, 111 . . . or more.	**Compromise, Fight, or Flight.** Ineffective people believe the whole is less than the sum of its parts. They try to "clone" other people in their own image. Differences in others are looked upon as threats.
HABIT 7	
Habit 7: Sharpen the Saw®. Effective people constantly renew themselves in the four basic areas of life: physical, social/emotional, mental, and spiritual. This increases their capacity to live all other habits of effectiveness.	**Wear Out the Saw.** Ineffective people lack a program of self-renewal and self-improvement, and eventually lose the cutting edge they may have once had.

SELF-SCORING 7 HABITS ASSESSMENT

This assessment will help you know where you are in living the 7 Habits and give you an idea of some of the areas you may want to focus on as you progress through this workbook. To help gauge your progress when you complete the workbook, you may retake this assessment.

On the following two pages, read each statement and, using your best judgment, circle the number that indicates how well you perform in each habit (1 being very poor and 6 being outstanding).

SELF-SCORING 7 HABITS ASSESSMENT						
EMOTIONAL BANK ACCOUNT						
1. I show kindness and consideration toward others.	1	2	3	4	5	6
2. I keep promises and honor commitments.	1	2	3	4	5	6
3. I do not speak negatively of others when they are not present.	1	2	3	4	5	6
P/PC BALANCE						
4. I am able to maintain an appropriate balance among the various aspects of my life—family, friends, work, and so forth.	1	2	3	4	5	6
5. When working on a task, I also keep in mind the concerns and needs of those I am working for.	1	2	3	4	5	6
6. I work hard at the things I do, but not in a manner that causes burnout.	1	2	3	4	5	6
HABIT 1: BE PROACTIVE						
7. I am in control of my life.	1	2	3	4	5	6
8. I focus my efforts on the things I can do something about rather than on the things beyond my control.	1	2	3	4	5	6
9. I take responsibility for my moods rather than blame others and circumstances.	1	2	3	4	5	6
HABIT 2: BEGIN WITH THE END IN MIND						
10. I know what I want to accomplish in my life.	1	2	3	4	5	6
11. I organize and prepare in a way that reduces having to work in a crisis mode.	1	2	3	4	5	6
12. I begin each week with a clear plan of what I desire to accomplish.	1	2	3	4	5	6

continued

SELF-SCORING 7 HABITS ASSESSMENT (continued)						
HABIT 3: PUT FIRST THINGS FIRST						
13. I am disciplined in carrying out plans (avoiding procrastination, time-wasters, and so forth).	1	2	3	4	5	6
14. I do not allow the truly important activities of my life to get lost in the busy activity of my days.	1	2	3	4	5	6
15. The things I do every day are meaningful and contribute to my overall goals in life.	1	2	3	4	5	6
HABIT 4: THINK WIN-WIN						
16. I care about the success of others as well as my own.	1	2	3	4	5	6
17. I cooperate with others.	1	2	3	4	5	6
18. When solving conflicts, I strive to find solutions that benefit all.	1	2	3	4	5	6
HABIT 5: SEEK FIRST TO UNDERSTAND, THEN TO BE UNDERSTOOD						
19. I am sensitive to the feelings of others.	1	2	3	4	5	6
20. I seek to understand the viewpoints of others.	1	2	3	4	5	6
21. When listening, I try to see things from the other person's point of view, not just from my own.	1	2	3	4	5	6
HABIT 6: SYNERGIZE						
22. I value and seek out the insights of others.	1	2	3	4	5	6
23. I am creative in searching for new and better ideas and solutions.	1	2	3	4	5	6
24. I encourage others to express their opinions.	1	2	3	4	5	6
HABIT 7: SHARPEN THE SAW						
25. I care for my physical health and well-being.	1	2	3	4	5	6
26. I strive to build and improve relationships with others.	1	2	3	4	5	6
27. I take time to find meaning and enjoyment in life.	1	2	3	4	5	6

CHARTING YOUR
7 HABITS EFFECTIVENESS

Total your points for each principle or habit in the Habit Totals column.

After you have computed your category totals, mark each score in the grid below and graph your totals. The higher your score, the more closely you are aligned with the 7 Habits principles.

	EMOTIONAL BANK ACCOUNT	P/PC BALANCE	HABIT 1	HABIT 2	HABIT 3	HABIT 4	HABIT 5	HABIT 6	HABIT 7
HABIT TOTALS									
Outstanding 18									
17									
16									
Very Good 15									
14									
13									
Good 12									
11									
10									
Fair 9									
8									
7									
Poor 6									
5									
4									
Very Poor 3									
2									
1									
0									

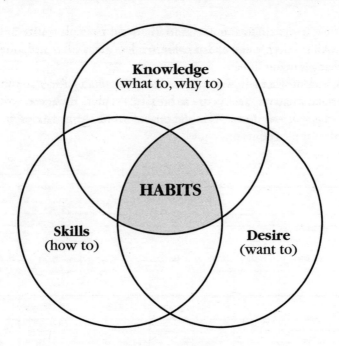

EFFECTIVE HABITS
Internalized principles and patterns of behavior

HABITS

A habit is the intersection of knowledge, skill, and desire. Knowledge is the *what to do* and the *why*. Skill is the *how to do*. Desire is the motivation—the *want to do*. All three of these things must come together in order to make a habit.

Think of two habits you have, one good and one bad. In the space below write down the knowledge, skills, and desires connected with those two habits.

_____

_____

_____

_____

_____

Habits have a tremendous pull—more than most people realize or will admit. Breaking a deeply embedded habit involves great effort and, oftentimes, major changes in our lives.

Look back at what you wrote down about your bad habit. Are you willing to undertake whatever is necessary to break that habit? If you are, write down three things you will do to begin the process of breaking that habit. Keep a record of your progress.

1. _____

_____

_____

_____

_____

2. _____

_____

_____

_____

_____

3. _____

_____

_____

_____

_____

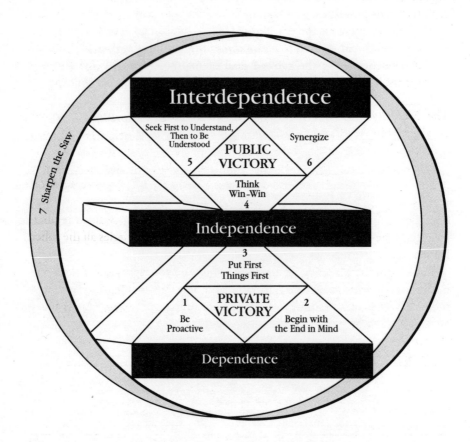

THE MATURITY CONTINUUM

THE MATURITY CONTINUUM®

The 7 Habits provide a sequential approach to move us progressively on a Maturity Continuum from dependence to independence to interdependence.

- Dependence is the paradigm of "you"—you take care of me.
- Independence is the paradigm of "I"—I am self-reliant.
- Interdependence is the paradigm of "we"—we can do it; we can combine our talents and abilities to create something greater together. Despite independence being the avowed goal of many people and social movements, interdependence is a far more effective and advanced concept.

The Maturity Continuum is built on an inside-out approach. In other words, Habits 1, 2, and 3 deal with self-mastery. They help you progress from dependence to independence, or the Private Victory®. As you become truly independent, you have the foundation for effective interdependence. You have the character base from which you can effectively work on Habits 4, 5, and 6—the more skill-oriented Public Victory® of teamwork, cooperation, and communication. Habit 7 is the habit of renewal—a regular, balanced renewal of the four basic dimensions of life. It encircles all the other habits.

Looking at the Maturity Continuum, where are you right now? Take a few minutes and record where you are now and why. What behaviors and attitudes do you exhibit that put you at this stage of the continuum? Are you beginning to see where you need the most work?

_____

_____

_____

_____

_____

_____

_____

_____

PART TWO

PRIVATE VICTORY®

HABIT 1

BE PROACTIVE®

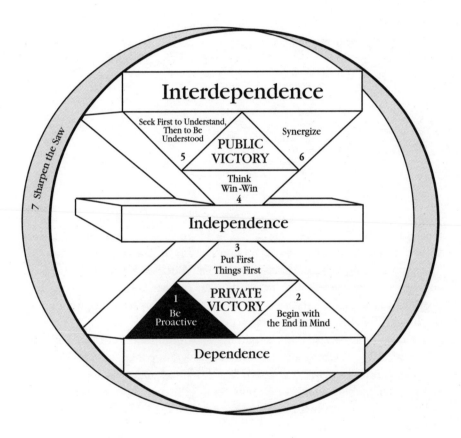

Before you begin this section of *The 7 Habits of Highly Effective People Personal Workbook*, read pages 66–94 in *The 7 Habits of Highly Effective People*.

HABIT 1: BE PROACTIVE

Life is a book and you are its author. You determine its plot and pace and you—only you—turn its pages.

—BETH MENDE CONNY

YOUR LIFE DOESN'T JUST "HAPPEN." Whether you know it or not, it is carefully designed by you—or carelessly designed by you. It is, after all, your choice. You choose happiness. You choose sadness. You choose decisiveness. You choose ambivalence. You choose success. You choose failure. You choose courage. You choose fear. Just remember that every moment, every situation, provides a new choice. And in doing so, it gives you a perfect opportunity to do things differently to produce more positive results.

Habit 1: Be Proactive is about taking responsibility for your life. You can't keep blaming everything on your parents or grandparents or your boss or coworkers, now, can you? Is your terrible childhood or genetics or work environment controlling your life? Or how about growing up poor—that's a great excuse for all your problems, isn't it? We do have the freedom to choose—all of us do.

Proactive people recognize that they are "response-able." They don't blame circumstances, conditions, or conditioning for their behavior. They know they choose their behavior. Reactive people, on the other hand, are often affected by their physical environment. If the weather is good, they feel good. If it isn't, it affects their attitude and performance.

Until we know ourselves and are aware of ourselves as separate from others and from the environment—until we can be separated even from ourselves so that we can observe our own tendencies, thoughts, and desires—we have no foundation from which to know and respect other people, let alone create change within ourselves. —STEPHEN R. COVEY

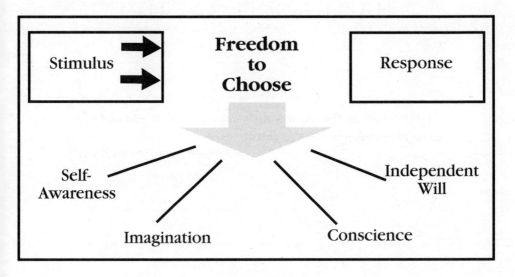

PROACTIVE MODEL

DEVELOPING PROACTIVITY
....

Between stimulus and response, you have the freedom to choose. This is your greatest power. One of the most important things you choose is what you say. Your language is a good indicator of how you see yourself. A proactive person uses proactive language—I can, I will, I prefer, etc. A reactive person uses reactive language—I can't, I must, if only. Reactive people believe they are not responsible for what they say—they have no choice.

   Think of two or three situations in your personal life during the past few weeks when you have responded in a reactive way. Describe what you *said*.

1. _____

_____

_____

_____

_____

2. _____

_____

_____

_____

_____

3. _____

_____

_____

_____

_____

Now think of some proactive responses you might have used in the same situations. Write them down in the spaces below.

1. _____

_____

_____

_____

2. _____

_____

_____

_____

_____

3. _____

_____

_____

_____

_____

Make it a point to really listen to your language during the next week. Is your language more proactive or reactive?

Is there an area in your life you are unhappy about or frustrated by—family, a relationship, your job?

What are you unhappy about or frustrated by? For example, do you feel powerless, hopeless, or used? Describe the situation.

_____

_____

_____

_____

_____

What is the stimulus to your frustration or unhappiness?

_____

_____

_____

_____

_____

How do you respond?

_____

_____

_____

_____

_____

What other choices might exist between the stimulus and the response?

_____

_____

_____

_____

_____

As this situation arises, remember your ability to choose your response and choose one of the responses you came up with in the question above.

You can MASTER the moment between a negative stimulus and your response by following these steps:

1. **M**easure how important the situation is to you on a scale of 1–5.
2. **A**ssess your initial reaction—frustration, anger, fear, etc.
3. **S**ee the stimulus/response model in your mind.
4. **T**hink about a proactive response.
5. **E**ngage or exit—use the response you've chosen or exit the situation.
6. **R**eview your performance to see how proactive you are.

Think of a recent situation (possibly the one you chose earlier) and take it through the MASTER steps.

Measure

_____

_____

_____

_____

Assess

_____

_____

_____

_____

See

_____

_____

_____

_____

_____

Think

_____

_____

_____

_____

_____

Engage or exit

_____

_____

_____

_____

_____

Review

_____

_____

_____

_____

_____

Would the outcome have been different if you had used this technique?

MASTER CHECKLIST	YOUR RESPONSE
Measure the importance.	
Assess your initial reaction.	
See the stimulus/response model.	
Think about a proactive response.	
Engage or exit.	
Review your performance.	

Use the MASTER checklist for one week. Make a conscious effort to use your "pause" button in the moment of choice and work toward proactive responses. Assess your progress at the end of the week by answering these questions:

1. What were the outcomes to my conscious, proactive responses?

_____

_____

_____

_____

_____

2. What would have been the outcomes had I chosen reactive responses?

_____

_____

_____

_____

_____

3. In what ways have my proactive responses improved my life?

_____

_____

_____

_____

_____

Remember that mastering proactive responses will take time and practice. You may not always succeed, but just remembering that you have a choice will make a great deal of difference.

HOW LARGE IS YOUR CIRCLE?

You have control over three things: what you think, what you say, and how you behave. To make a change in your life, you must recognize these gifts are the most powerful tools you possess in shaping the form of your life.
—SONYA FRIEDMAN

The problems, challenges, and opportunities we face each day fall into two areas: Circle of Concern and Circle of Influence. We each have a wide range of concerns—our health, our children, problems at work, the national debt, terrorism in the world, the weather. As we look at this list, it becomes apparent that there are some things over which we have no real control and others that we can do something about. Proactive people focus their efforts on their Circle of Influence. They work on the things they can do something about: health, children, problems at work. Reactive people focus their efforts in the Circle of Concern, things over which they have little or no control: the national debt, terrorism, the weather. Gaining an awareness of in which area we expend our energies is a giant step in developing proactivity.

During this week, write down the various challenges and problems you face. Which area does each fall within? What is your immediate response?

CHALLENGE/PROBLEM	AREA	RESPONSE
Traffic jam on the way home	Circle of concern	Anger, swearing

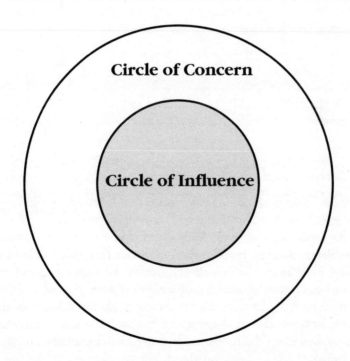

Keeping in mind the above model and making your Circle of Influence grow, choose one challenge from each of the areas above that you would like to work on during the next week. How will you change your response to meet the challenge more effectively?

1. Circle of Influence

_____

_____

_____

_____

_____

2. Circle of Concern

_____

_____

_____

_____

_____

TAKING INITIATIVE

Demosthenes, one of Aristotle's contemporaries, desperately wanted to be a public speaker. But his inarticulate and stammering pronunciation made attaining his dream seem unlikely. Through conscious endeavor, Demosthenes overcame his limitations. He learned to speak distinctly by talking with pebbles in his mouth, and further trained his voice by speaking and reciting speeches while breathlessly running up and down stairs.

Is there something you have always wanted to do but felt you didn't have the talent, time, or ability? What would it take for you to overcome your weaknesses? What one thing can you do this week to begin?

_____

_____

_____

_____

_____

Have you ever tried to put the skids on an ant? It's virtually impossible. They never stop. Put one to the test someday. Pretend you're five years old again, and make a little hill in an ant's path. The ant will walk up and over the top without braking. It will go into a hole, over a log, through grass. If it can't go through, it will go around. An ant will never turn around and walk the other way, no matter what obstacles are in its path.

Try applying that tenacity to your life. Of course, you'll want to use your brain, too. But in the determination department, be an ant. Refuse to be stopped. Keep going, make proactive choices, and learn as you go. People who patiently persist finally see their dreams come true.

Got Courage?!

If you could develop a new talent, what would it be?

_____

_____

_____

_____

_____

If you could travel to anywhere in the world, where would it be?

_____

_____

_____

_____

_____

If you could change one thing about your life, what would it be?

_____

_____

_____

_____

_____

What's stopping you from doing any or all of these things? You have the choice, don't you? What would it be like if you lived your life as a work of art in progress? If each breath and each action were part of an unfolding masterpiece? If you saw the shadows and light areas as part of the composition? Accepted it all? Found joy in the beauty of it?

Where are your choices taking you? What you make of your life is up to you. Every person creates his or her own reality. Authorship of your life is one of your absolute rights, yet so often people deny that they have the ability to script the life they desire. They look past the fundamental truth that it is not our external resources that determine our success or failure, but rather our own belief in ourselves and our willingness to create a life according to our highest aspirations.

Got Courage?!

Use the space below to record your plan for implementing ways to make your answers to the questions on pages 37 and 38 come to fruition.

_____

_____

HABIT 2

BEGIN WITH THE
END IN MIND®

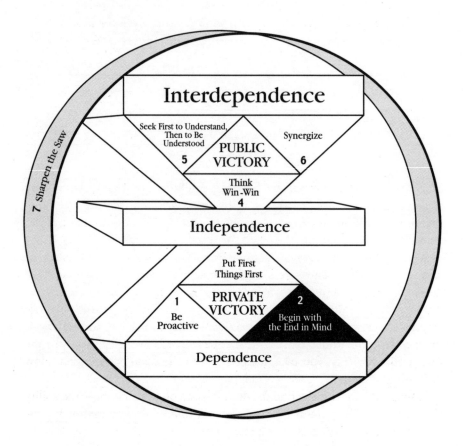

Before you begin this section of *The 7 Habits of Highly Effective People Personal Workbook*,
read pages 96–144 in *The 7 Habits of Highly Effective People*.

HABIT 2: BEGIN WITH THE END IN MIND

Imagining what you want as if it already exists opens the door to letting it happen.
                                            —SHAKTI GAWAIN

So, WHAT DO YOU WANT to be when you grow up? That question may appear a little trite at first, but just think about it for a moment. Are you— right now—who you want to be, what you dreamed you'd be, doing what you always wanted to do? Now, be honest. Well, are you?

It's incredibly easy to get caught up in the activity trap, in the "busyness" of life, to work harder and harder at climbing the ladder of success, only to discover, upon reaching the top rung, that the ladder is leaning against the wrong wall. Sometimes people find themselves achieving victories that are empty—successes that have come at the expense of things they suddenly real- ize were far more valuable to them. If your ladder is not leaning against the right wall, every step you take just gets you to the wrong place faster. How depressing is that?

Habit 2: Begin with the End in Mind is based on imagination—the ability to envision, see the potential, create with our minds what we cannot at pres- ent see with our eyes and conscience. It is based on the principle that all things are created twice. There is a mental (or first) creation and a physical (or second) creation. The second creation follows from the first, just as a build- ing follows from a blueprint. It's the same in your personal life. If you don't make a conscious effort to visualize who you are and what you want in life, then you empower other people and circumstances to shape you and your life by default. It's about connecting again with your own uniqueness and then defining the personal, moral, and ethical guidelines within which you can most happily express and fulfill it. To begin with the end in mind means to begin each day, task, or project with a clear vision of your desired direction and destination, and then continue by flexing your proactive muscles to make things happen.

CHECKING YOUR VISION

It's time for a personal vision checkup. Take a minute and think about each question below. Write your thoughts in the space provided.

What am I doing right now with my life? Does it make me happy? Do I feel fulfilled?

_____

_____

_____

_____

_____

What do I keep gravitating toward? Is it different from what I am currently doing?

_____

_____

_____

_____

_____

What did I like to do as a child? Do those things still bring me satisfaction? Am I doing any of them?

_____

_____

_____

_____

_____

What interests me most right now?

_____

_____

_____

_____

_____

What fills my soul?

_____

_____

_____

_____

_____

What can I do well? What are my unique traits and strengths?

_____

_____

_____

_____

_____

DEVELOPING A
PERSONAL MISSION STATEMENT®

One of the best ways to begin with the end in mind and incorporate Habit 2 into your life is to develop a Personal Mission Statement. It focuses on what you want to be and do. It is your plan for success. It reaffirms who you are, puts your goals in focus, and moves your ideas into the real world. Your mission statement makes you the leader of your own life. You create your own destiny and secure the future you envision. How about that? Look again at your responses to the questions in Checking Your Vision on pages 42 and 43. It's very likely that your true mission in life is beginning to surface again.

Let's get to work on your Personal Mission Statement. The sooner you have a clear vision of what you want to be and the contributions you want to make, the more effective you'll be in your life. Keep in mind that a Personal Mission Statement is, well, personal. There is no set length or style. It can be a poem, a few sentences, a few pages, or even a song. As a sculptor must bring shape, color, and expression to his clay, the same is true of your mission statement. You bring your past experiences, wisdom, ideas, and creativity to the process of creating a Personal Mission Statement. If what you write feels flat and unexciting, you're on the wrong track. If the words overwhelm you with emotion and excitement, you're onto something!

Beginning on the next page are six steps that will help you develop a Personal Mission Statement.

Step 1: Brainstorm Ideas

In the space provided, write about each of the three topics below without stopping. This is freewriting, so don't worry about spelling, punctuation, etc. If you hit a point where you can't think of anything to write, just keep going and write and words or phrases that come immediately to mind. Remember, you're brainstorming and not writing a final draft. The purpose is to capture your ideas on paper. Spend two to three minutes on each question.

1. *Identify an influential person.*
Identify one person who had (knowingly or unknowingly) a positive influence on your life. What are the qualities you most admire in this person? What qualities did you gain from this person?

_____

_____

_____

_____

_____

_____

_____

_____

2. *Define who you want to become.*
Imagine it's twenty years in the future. You have achieved all you ever hoped to achieve. What is your list of accomplishments? What do you want to have, do, and be?

_____

_____

_____

_____

_____

_____

_____

_____

_____

_____

3. *Determine what is important to you today.*
   What are the ten things that are most rewarding to you today? What do you live for and love in life?

_____

_____

_____

_____

_____

_____

_____

_____

_____

Step 2: Take a Breather

Now take a deep breath and relax. Put your writing aside for a few minutes and walk away from it.

Step 3: Gather Your Thoughts

Review what you've written and circle the key ideas, words, and phrases that you would like to include in your mission statement.

Step 4: Write a Rough Draft

Now it's time to write a rough draft of your mission statement. There are some Personal Mission Statement examples on pages 50 and 51 to help get you thinking. During the week, carry your rough draft with you and make notes, additions, and deletions as needed each day. You may wish to write a new draft each day or every other day. This is an ongoing exercise. Your mission statement will change over time as you change. Take some time right now and compose a rough draft of your mission statement.

MISSION STATEMENT ROUGH DRAFT

_____

_____

_____

_____

_____

_____

_____

_____

_____

_____

_____

_____

_____

_____

_____

_____

_____

Step 5: Complete Your Mission Statement

At the end of the week, write a final copy of your mission statement and find a permanent place for it where you can easily access it. If you would like, you can compose your Personal Mission Statement below and then tear it out.

MY MISSION STATEMENT

_____

_____

_____

_____

_____

_____

_____

_____

_____

_____

_____

_____

_____

_____

_____

_____

_____

_____

_____

Step 6: Periodically Review and Evaluate

Every month or so ask yourself the following questions:

- Do I feel that this mission statement represents the best within me?
- Do I feel direction, purpose, challenge, and motivation when I review my mission statement?
- Am I living my life according to the ideals and values that are incorporated in my mission statement?

PERSONAL MISSION
STATEMENT EXAMPLES

EXAMPLE 1

My life is an adventure to savor and enjoy. I have a great purpose and destiny. In my life I will:

Love and serve God, family, and neighbors.

Have joy in serving.

Build and strengthen young people.

Seek truth.

Develop wisdom.

Teach.

Set an example.

Share.

Have health and strength.

Be faithful.

Walk in peace.

Pray.

Listen.

Be patient.

Cultivate peace and harmony.

Honor my mother.

Remember who I am, where I came from, and my purpose.

Example 2

My mission is to give, for giving is what I do best, and I can learn to do better. I will seek to learn, for learning is the basis for growth, and growing is the key to living. I will seek first to understand, for understanding is the key to finding value, and value is the basis for respect, decisions, and action. This should be my first act with my wife, my family, and my business. I want to help influence the future development of people and organizations. I want to teach my children and others to love and laugh, to learn and grow beyond their current bounds. I will build personal, business, and civic relationships by giving in frequent little ways.

Example 3

> To cultivate a universal responsibility for one another and the planet we
> share.   —THE DALAI LAMA

ROLES AND GOALS

Now that you have a rough draft of your Personal Mission Statement in progress, it's important to consider the roles and goals in your life and how they relate to your mission statement. Roles and goals give structure and organized direction to your personal mission. We'll tackle roles first.

Roles

You live your life in terms of roles—not in the sense of role-playing, but in the sense of authentic relationships and responsibilities you've committed to. You may have important roles in your family, in the community, at work, or in other areas of your life. Roles represent responsibilities, relationships, and areas of contribution.

You may define your family role as simply "family member." Or you may choose to divide it into roles such as "partner" and "parent." Your profession or work life may contain several roles. For example, you may have one role in administration and another in marketing. It's up to you to define your roles in a way that works for you.

In the space provided on the next page, write your roles. Don't be too concerned about getting them "right" the first time. Just write the ones that feel right for you. Try to limit the number of roles on your list to seven or less. If you have more than seven, combine some functions to get down to seven or less. Next to the role, write a description of what optimal performance in that role would look like for you.

Sample Roles:

Artist	Caregiver	Companion	Director	Energizer
Friend	Grandparent	Inventor	Neighbor	Peacemaker
Son	Teacher	Trainer	Volunteer	Writer

ROLE	STATEMENT OF OPTIMAL PERFORMANCE IN ROLE
Sample: Volunteer	Sample: Spend 2 hours at Children's Center—3/21

When you identify your roles, you create a variety of perspectives from which to examine your life. As you incorporate your goals into your mission statement, you give balance and harmony to your life.

Goals

Now that you've identified your roles, it's time to think about the goals that surround your mission. Goals are what give your mission statement momentum. They create a plan of action and help measure whether or not you are successfully living your mission statement. Many of the goals that flow from your mission statement will be long-term. Short-term goals, such as weekly goals, are important to your mission statement as well, and we'll explore those further in Habit 3.

Let's Set Some Goals

Think of goals you've had in the past. Did your success have anything to do with your mission? Chances are, if the goal wasn't connected to something important, it didn't get done. Take a few minutes and review your mission statement. Don't worry if it's still a rough draft. In the space provided below, create three long-term goals that support your mission.

Long-term goal 1

Long-term goal 2

Long-term goal 3

REALIZING YOUR GOALS

What? Why? How? When? These might seem like simple words and concepts, but when applied to your goals, they bring them into focus and closer to reality. With every goal you set, it's important to ask yourself what, why, how, and when.

What?

First of all, congratulations! You've already completed the first step of manifesting your goals: the "what." You've already created three long-term goals. You've named three goals that will bring your life into alignment with what you have decreed is your greater purpose. (If you haven't created three long-term goals yet, stop right where you are and go back to Let's Set Some Goals, on page 53.)

Why?

Try to articulate why a particular goal will serve what you believe in. Why do you wish to see this goal fulfilled? Why is it important to you and your mission? Often there are clues and secrets that will be revealed when doing this. Many times people who might be able to help you, and the things you will need in order to achieve what you desire, become apparent when this exploration is undertaken. Asking yourself "why" brings clarity to your goals. Clarity is a key toward determination and action.

Take some time right now to determine why the three long-term goals you've identified are important to you.

Why long-range goal 1 is important to me:

_____

_____

_____

_____

_____

Why long-range goal 2 is important to me:

_____

_____

_____

_____

_____

Why long-range goal 3 is important to me:

_____

_____

_____

_____

_____

How?

When you have tackled what and why, the next step is "how." How will you know when you have arrived? How will you get there? How will you mark the way to seeing your goal realized? How are you going to get it done? How will you empower yourself to achieve your goal? Taking the time to visualize and feel the "how" helps you see some of the necessary steps to take in order to achieve your goal. This is perhaps the most critical step in making that all-important transition: transforming your goals from merely ideas and dreams into concrete reality. The more thoroughly you do this, the easier it will be to make a list of the realistic steps it will take to get you where you'd like to be. Take a look at this example:

> A father decides he'd like to improve his relationship with his son as one of his goals. His son has faced a lot of challenges lately: the boy's schoolwork is poor, and he's fallen in with a questionable crowd of friends. The father loves his son and feels their relationship could be stronger. He's clear about his "what" and his "why." Now for the big "how."

> How do I intend to improve my relationship with my son?

By looking for opportunities. (But how?)

By investing time. (Okay. How?)

By setting aside specific time. (How will you go about that?)

By making time in my schedule just for him. (Sounds good. How?)

By finding a day where he and I can go and do something special. (Cool. How?)

By deciding on an event, and taking him with me. (Great! How?)

By going hiking this Saturday. (Sounds like a great plan! But still, how?)

By making sure he is free; by committing to the plan and sticking with it. (Excellent! Any more "hows"?)

By committing to a time each week to find something just for us to do and sticking with it. (Brilliant. Um, how?)

By telling him I would like for this to happen so he knows and can begin to be part of the planning process as well. (Awesome. How?)

By committing to being open to his suggestions for things to do so I can really begin to understand his interests and ideas. (How many kids can say this is "how" their father figures in their lives? Pretty amazing stuff here!)

TELL YOURSELF HOW

Choose one of your long-term goals and play the "how" game. Make a list indicating how you are going to achieve your goal. Every time you write down a "how," ask yourself exactly how that "how" will manifest itself. Don't let yourself off the hook so easily! Push yourself. Get specific. Demand your success!

Long-term goal _____

_____ *How?*

_____ *How?*

_____ *How?*

_____ *How?*

_____ _How?_

_____ _How?_

_____ _How?_

_____ _How?_

_____ _How?_

_____ _How?_

_____ _How?_

_____ _How?_

_____ _How?_

When?

You've probably heard people talk about cramming the night before an exam or presentation, working well under pressure, meeting tight deadlines. Deadlines? They can be stressful at times, but they mean business, and people respond to them. So what about your goals? Why can't your dreams have deadlines? What if you took your goals as seriously as, let's say, a project at work or a job for a client? Aren't your aspirations just as important, if not more important?

You know where you're at right now, and you know where you want to go. Now, when do you want to be there? It's time to give your long-term goals a deadline. Turn back to page 53 and set a deadline for each of your long-term goals.

Now that you have a deadline set for your three long-term goals, let's dig a little deeper. Let's narrow your focus to the goal you selected for the "how" game. Before you set out on a journey, you need to know what the path looks like. Are there many steps involved with this goal, or does it require a few major milestones? In the space provided on the next page, start brainstorming all the steps involved. This means everything from phone calls to budgets to delegating tasks. You may need to purchase things, talk to advisors, or do some networking. What is it going to take to get you from here to there? Take a look back at your "how" list. You may have identified some of the steps already!

What are the steps that will take me to my goal?

_____

_____

_____

_____

_____

_____

_____

_____

_____

_____

What good are directions if they aren't in some kind of order? Take a look at the steps in your list and prioritize them to the best of your ability. Which things must come before others? Which ones can wait until farther down the road? Take an inventory of what's there and give it a whirl.

GET IT TOGETHER!

Now it's time to bring it all together. On the opposite page you'll see a goal-planning tool. In the section marked Long-Term Goal (What), write the name of the goal you selected for the "how" game. In the space marked Deadline (When), write the deadline you selected. In the section Impor-

GOAL PLANNING

Long-Term Goal (What): _____

_____

_____

_____

_____ Deadline (When): _____

Importance to Mission/Role (Why): _____

_____

_____

	Steps (How)	Deadlines (When)

tance to Mission/Roles (Why), summarize your "why" responses. In the section Steps (How), list the goal steps in the order you prioritized them. And finally, in the Deadlines (When) column to the right, try to give each step a potential deadline.

Now it's up to you! With the what, why, how, and when identified for your goal, you're on your way to success. You can use this same process with all of your goals. Since you've broken your goal into steps, you can now schedule those steps into your week, your day, and even the present moment. What can you get done today, tomorrow, or next week that will bring you that much closer to your final destination? See if you can project a bit and schedule just the first three steps on your list into your planning system. The rest will come later. Then go for it! Move ahead each day with the vision of that goal in mind and keep pressing forward.

HABIT 3

PUT FIRST
THINGS FIRST®

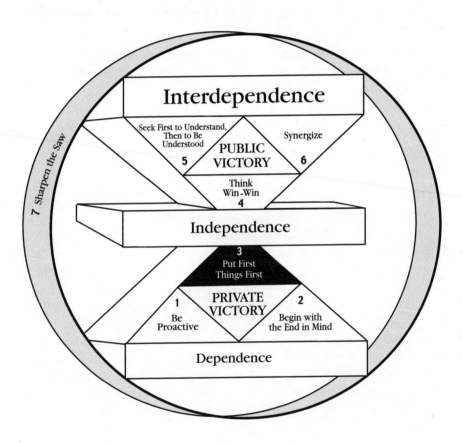

Before you begin this section of *The 7 Habits of Highly Effective People Personal Workbook*,
read pages 145–182 in *The 7 Habits of Highly Effective People*.

HABIT 3: PUT FIRST THINGS FIRST

Each day has its own purpose and fits into the great plan of our lives. This very moment carries traces of our life purpose in places where we focus our attention, in words or ideas that bring a tingle of excitement and hope in our heart.
—CAROL ADRIENNE

IN ORDER TO LIVE a more balanced life, you have to recognize that not doing everything that comes along is okay. There's no need to over-extend yourself anymore. All it takes is realizing that it's all right to say no when necessary and then focus on your highest priorities. But before you can move ahead, you need to become clear about who you are and what you really want.

Habit 1 says, "You're in charge. You're the creator." Being proactive is about choice. Habit 2 is the first, or mental, creation. Beginning with the end in mind is about vision. Habit 3 is the second creation, the physical creation. This habit is where Habits 1 and 2 come together. It's day-in and day-out, moment-by-moment, doing it. It deals with many of the questions addressed in the field of time management. But that's not all it's about. Habit 3 is about life management as well—your purpose, values, roles, and priorities.

FIRST THINGS?

What are "first things"? First things are those things you, personally, find most worth doing. If you put first things first, you are organizing and manag-

ing time and events according to the personal priorities you established in
Habit 2.

> *The successful person has the habit of doing things failures don't like to do.*
> *They don't like doing them either necessarily. But their disliking is subordi-*
> *nated to the strength of their purpose.* —*ALBERT E. N. GRAY*

Basically, we spend our time in one of four ways, as illustrated in the Time
Matrix™ below. This matrix defines activities as "urgent" or "not urgent,"
and "important" or "not important." Let's see where you spend most of your
time.

THE TIME MANAGEMENT MATRIX	
URGENT	NOT URGENT
I ACTIVITIES: Crises Pressing problems Deadline-driven projects	II ACTIVITIES: Prevention, PC activities Relationship building Recognizing new opportunities Planning, recreation
III ACTIVITIES: Interruptions, some calls Some mail, some reports Some meetings Proximate, pressing matters Popular activities	IV ACTIVITIES: Trivia, busy work Some mail Some phone calls Time wasters Pleasant activities

(Left margin labels: IMPORTANT for rows I & II; NOT IMPORTANT for rows III & IV)

THE TIME MATRIX
QUICK ASSESSMENT

This tool is designed to give you a quick estimate of the relative amount of time
and energy you spend in each of the quadrants of the Time Matrix. Circle your
response from 1 to 6 to each of the eight questions on the next page.

Questions	Strongly Disagree	Disagree	Slightly Disagree	Slightly Agree	Agree	Strongly Agree
1. I spend much of my time on important activities that demand my immediate attention, such as crises, pressing problems, and deadline-driven projects.	1	2	3	4	5	6
2. I feel I am always "putting out fires" and working in a crisis mode.	1	2	3	4	5	6
3. I feel as if I waste a lot of time.	1	2	3	4	5	6
4. I spend much of my time on activities that have little relevance to my top priorities but demand my immediate attention (e.g., needless interruptions, unimportant meetings, noncritical phone calls, and e-mail).	1	2	3	4	5	6
5. I spend much of my time on activities that are impor-tant but not urgent, such as planning, preparation, pre-vention, relationship building, and self-renewal.	1	2	3	4	5	6
6. I spend much of my time on busywork, compulsive habits, junk mail, excessive TV, Internet trivia, games, etc.	1	2	3	4	5	6
7. I feel I am on top of things because of careful preparation, planning, and prevention.	1	2	3	4	5	6
8. I feel I am constantly addressing issues that are important to others but not to me.	1	2	3	4	5	6

SCORING

Instructions:

1. Circle your response 1–6 to each of the eight questions on the previous page.
2. For each quadrant, add your responses for the questions indicated.
3. Fill in the area in each quadrant up to the number that corresponds to the total.

EXAMPLE:

Question 1 = 2
Question 2 = 4
Total = 6

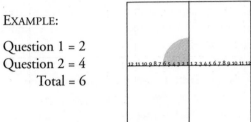

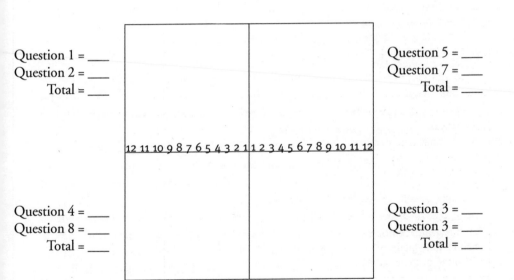

Question 1 = ___
Question 2 = ___
Total = ___

Question 5 = ___
Question 7 = ___
Total = ___

12 11 10 9 8 7 6 5 4 3 2 1 | 1 2 3 4 5 6 7 8 9 10 11 12

Question 4 = ___
Question 8 = ___
Total = ___

Question 3 = ___
Question 3 = ___
Total = ___

Highly effective people do not really manage time—they manage themselves. While most of the world spins around in Quadrant I, reacting to urgent matters and managing one crisis after another, people who spend a majority of their time in Quadrant II are leading balanced, serene, and ordered lives. They are planning and executing according to their highest priorities.

Highly effective people are able to manage themselves so well in relation to the precious resource of time because they live the 7 Habits, which are

Quadrant II activities. Everyone deals with fundamentally important things that, if done on a regular basis, would make a profound difference in the quality of their lives.

THE 7 HABITS—
QUADRANT II ACTIVITIES

Habit 1: Be Proactive®. Quadrant II has to be acted upon proactively, as opposed to Quadrants I and III, which are reacted to. In Quadrant II, individuals realize, "I am not a product of limited time; rather I am a product of my chosen responses to circumstances."

Habit 2: Begin with the End in Mind®. Another Quadrant II activity is to take the time and initiative to develop a mission statement based on principles. A good mission statement is the key that effective people use to discern which things are important—which things are really worth acting upon. People who spend most of their time in Quadrants I and III begin with no particular objective in mind, sailing through life with no map, no compass, and limited vision.

Habit 3: Put First Things First®. Habit 3 is the essence of Quadrant II—putting first those things that are important and in line with one's mission statement. This habit represents the process of completing tasks according to one's highest priorities. People who spend their time in Quadrants I and III put second things first, reacting to pressing, popular, pleasant, and proximate things.

Habit 4: Think Win-Win®. Forming Win-Win agreements is also a Quadrant II activity. Not only does it take real effort, it also requires good communication skills and a high trust level. Quadrants III and IV may lead to just the opposite: Win-Lose or Lose-Win.

Habit 5: Seek First to Understand, Then to Be Understood®. People with a Quadrant I mind-set want to do only the expedient thing—to be understood. This mind-set inevitably leads to conflict and a breakdown of communication. On the other hand, those with a Quadrant II mind-set subordinate their desire to be heard in order to first understand. Understanding requires perceptive observation and empathic listening, and is the essence of effective communication—a Quadrant II activity.

Habit 6: Synergize®. In Quadrant I, people function independently of others. They resist input from others, and their focus is on efficiency—getting the job done while minimizing conflict. The result is usually an inferior product or a mediocre service. Conversely, a person with a Quadrant II mind-set actively seeks feedback from people who see things differently from how he or she does, resulting in a better solution or a higher-quality product or service.

Habit 7: Sharpen the Saw®. Since the habit of self-renewal is not urgent and takes time, most people neglect it. Taking time to Sharpen the Saw is a fundamental Quadrant II activity that affects all the other habits. Spending time on personal development, prevention, relationship building, and planning are examples of Quadrant II activities, and require action.

MY PRIORITIES AND
HOW I SPEND MY TIME

Review your mission statement, roles and goals, and current weekly plan. What are your top three priorities for this week? These are your Quadrant II activities. Write them below.

1. _____

2. _____

3. _____

THE TIME MANAGEMENT MATRIX	
URGENT	NOT URGENT
I	II
III	IV

IMPORTANT

NOT IMPORTANT

During the next week, keep track of how you are spending your time. In the Time Matrix above, write the activities that belong in each quadrant.

Did you meet your Quadrant II priorities? If not, why not?

_____

_____

_____

_____

_____

In the space below, decide on a plan for how you will better meet those Quadrant II priorities next week. Write your plan in your chosen planning tool and schedule any appropriate tasks and appointments.

_____

_____

_____

_____

_____

PURPOSE

So, now you know where you are spending most of your time. Are you interested in raising the bar? Are you interested in pulling yourself out of Quadrants I, III, and IV and into Quadrant II? Let's figure out how you can do that.

Sometimes in your life you will go on a journey. It will be the longest journey you have ever taken. It is the journey to find yourself.

—KATHERINE SHARP

Where is your journey taking you? What little issues are blocking your energy? What is your purpose? Take a few minutes to write down your thoughts about where you are in your journey.

_____

_____

_____

_____

Don't feel as if you are out of the ordinary if you struggle with this. Many people do. Many times, thinking about what your "first things" are can help move you along the path. Keeping your first things in mind, respond to the following questions:

1. Do you really want to pursue and follow your purpose? If so, why? If not, why not?

_____

_____

_____

_____

_____

2. What is and isn't working in your life?

_____

_____

_____

_____

_____

3. What do you want to change about your life?

_____

_____

_____

_____

_____

4. Before you become overwhelmed, list some *small* changes you can make right now instead of trying to take on everything at once.

_____

_____

_____

_____

_____

5. Now that you've written down some of the "right now" things you can do, create several realistic, long-term goals and strategies that will move you forward on your journey. You may want to refer back to your goals from Habit 2.

_____

_____

_____

_____

_____

6. How are you going to hold yourself accountable for following through on your goals and strategies?

_____

_____

_____

_____

_____

Remember to listen to your inner voice to guide you along the path. Forget about what others think of your desire to change. Believe that anything is possible when you're "on purpose." Realize that everything happens for a reason when it is supposed to happen, but it's up to you to make it or break it!

VALUES

When you were answering the questions about your purpose, did you find that some of your values cropped up? That's not surprising when you consider that your purpose is, in some ways, driven by your values. Time and life management (fourth-generation time management) recognizes that people are more important than things. It helps give direction and purpose to the way you spend each day. Do you live what you believe?

> *You are a disciple, a follower, of your own deep values and their source. And you have the will, the integrity, to subordinate your feelings, your impulses, your moods to those values.* —STEPHEN R. COVEY

Answer the following questions and explore any recurring themes.

1. What do you want to contribute?

_____

_____

_____

_____

_____

2. What interests you most?

_____

_____

_____

_____

3. What do you feel passionate about?

_____

_____

_____

_____

4. What is important to you?

_____

_____

_____

_____

_____

5. What do you want to accomplish?

_____

_____

_____

_____

_____

6. What do you believe in?

_____

_____

_____

_____

_____

7. What is your potential?

_____

_____

_____

_____

_____

8. What do you stand for?

_____

_____

_____

_____

_____

9. What values are most important to you?

_____

_____

_____

_____

_____

Are you beginning to get a feel for where you stand, what you value, and what your purpose is? It's never easy to take a good, hard look at one's life. Believing in something makes it possible. It doesn't necessarily make it easy. Going through this process will help you have a clear knowledge and understanding of what your highest priorities really are. The next step is to look at the roles you play and how you can balance them all.

ROLES

There comes a point in many people's lives when they can no longer play the role they have chosen for themselves. When that happens, we are like actors finding that someone has changed the play. —BRIAN MOORE

In Habit 2, you listed the roles you play each day. How do your roles tie in with Habit 3 and your first things? With your purpose and values? As you plan your week using your chosen planning tool, be sure you schedule activities in each key role.

Make a list of your key roles and jot down an activity you will schedule in the coming week for each of them. Remember, you may not have a specific task or appointment assigned for each role. You may list something such as

"Be a better listener" under your role as parent. The key question is, "What is the most important thing you can do in this role this week?"

1. _____

_____

_____

_____

2. _____

_____

_____

_____

3. _____

_____

_____

_____

4. _____

_____

_____

_____

_____

5. _____

_____

_____

_____

_____

6. _____

_____

_____

_____

_____

7. _____

_____

_____

_____

_____

Now transfer what you've written to your Weekly Compass® if you're using a Franklin Planning System, or to an appropriate place in another planning tool.

PRIORITIES
....

The key is not to prioritize what's on your schedule, but to schedule your priorities.　　　　　　　　　　　　　—STEPHEN R. COVEY

Scheduling your life around your highest priorities may seem daunting. In reality, it's a simple, clear process that will move you forward on your journey—*if* you are clear about your priorities first!

What are your top five priorities? List them below.

1. _____

2. _____

3. _____

4. _____

5. _____

Is it realistic to think you can accomplish all five of the priorities you listed above? Have you thought about delegating anything?

Some people think of delegation as giving up control or admitting you "can't do it all." Well, so what if you can't do it all? The reality is that no one can do it all with excellence all of the time. Delegating to qualified others frees you up to put your energy into the things that are truly your highest priorities.

Look back at the list of your five highest priorities. Take a few minutes to really think about them and then prioritize them in order of importance. Write the list again below.

1. _____

2. _____

3. _____

4. _____

5. _____

Now look at your fourth and fifth priorities. Decide how you could delegate at least a small part of each to someone else so that those things continue to move forward with minimal effort on your part. Write your plan below.

_____

_____

_____

_____

_____

Is there anything in the first three that could be delegated as well? Record it below.

_____

_____

_____

_____

_____

Effectively delegating to others is perhaps the single most powerful high-leverage activity there is. —STEPHEN R. COVEY

TRUST
....

Did you just go through the last exercise thinking there's no one you can trust to do those things? You may think it's faster and easier to do it yourself, but does that allow others to grow and develop?

It takes time and patience to develop trust in others. If you are striving toward "stewardship delegation" rather than "gofer delegation," then everyone involved wins. Invest the time teaching, training, and exercising patience now, and the end result will be more time saved in the long run.

Refer back to the things you chose to delegate to someone else. What kind of delegation did you assign—stewardship or gofer?

_____

_____

_____

_____

_____

Now look at your list from the perspective of stewardship delegation. Begin building trust by offering opportunities for growth. What changes will you make to your delegation? Record the changes below and then move forward on them.

_____

_____

_____

_____

_____

WEEKLY PLANNING

So far, you've figured out your purpose, values, roles, and first things. How are you going to make sure your first things really are first and stay first? The best way we've found is through weekly planning.

There are many different tools you can choose to use for your personal planning system. At FranklinCovey, we realize you have many options—paper-based, handheld, and desktop, to name a few.

Your chosen tool should help you keep balance in your life by helping you identify your roles and priorities. You need a tool that will help you focus not only daily, which is a great thing, but weekly as well.

Organizing weekly helps keep you in the fourth generation of time and life management. It provides a larger context than simple daily planning. Truly scheduling your priorities can best be done from a weekly perspective.

As you move forward in keeping your first things first, commit to investing from twenty to thirty minutes a week in weekly planning. Follow these steps as you plan:

1. Write down your key roles.
2. Select one or two of your highest priorities to focus on this week.
3. Look at the week and schedule your tasks and appointments.
4. Adapt daily, using A, B, C, 1, 2, 3 prioritization.

PART THREE

PUBLIC VICTORY®

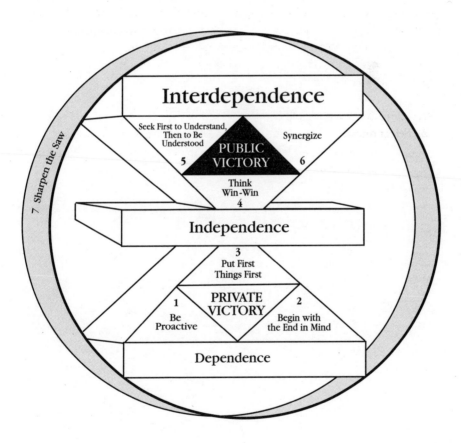

Before you begin this section of *The 7 Habits of Highly Effective People Personal Workbook*, read pages 185–203 in *The 7 Habits of Highly Effective People*.

LET'S TAKE INVENTORY

TAKE A LOOK BACK FOR A MOMENT and survey the terrain you've traveled so far. Remember that the seven Habits are based on a process called the inside-out approach. The first three habits concentrate on the "inside" portion of this process. So, in other words, you've been thinking only about yourself up until this point. And hasn't it felt good? You've been building and improving your relationship with yourself—your own character.

Habits 1, 2, and 3 have increased your self-respect and self-discipline, and have led you to a Private Victory of independence. Instead of feeling victimized and immobile, focusing on the weaknesses of other people and circumstances you believe are responsible for your current situation, you instead consciously choose to focus on your highest priorities and values—envisioning how you can best lead your life around those priorities and formulating a plan to execute on those priorities. Simply put, self-mastery is the foundation of good relationships with others. You can't be successful with other people if you haven't paid the price of success with yourself. Now, that's a paradigm shift!

After experiencing your Private Victory, Habits 4, 5, and 6 will lead you to a Public Victory of interdependence, where you will be capable of building rich, enduring, highly productive relationships with other people. It's now time to concentrate on the "out" of inside out.

EMOTIONAL BANK ACCOUNT®

Before you move on to Habits 4, 5, and 6, we'd like to introduce you to a powerful metaphor that effectively describes relationships. It's called the Emotional Bank Account.

DEPOSITS (+)	WITHDRAWALS (−)
Displaying kindness and courtesy	Displaying unkindness and discourtesy
Keeping promises	Breaking promises
Clear expectations	Unclear expectations
Loyalty to the absent	Showing disloyalty or duplicity
Apologizing	Having pride, conceit, or arrogance

The Emotional Bank Account is a metaphor that describes the amount of trust you build up in a relationship. Much like a financial bank account, deposits are made and withdrawals are taken from an Emotional Bank Account. When you do something positive for another person, it can be a major deposit for that person. Deposits build a reserve of goodwill and trust. On the other hand, when you do something negative toward another person, you make a withdrawal. When withdrawals exceed deposits, the account is overdrawn and the level of trust deteriorates. With your relationships, it's vital that you make continual deposits in order to sustain a high level of trust. The following are common emotional deposits and withdrawals:

TWO KEYS TO MAKING DEPOSITS

☞ Key 1:
Deposits need to be frequent and consistent.

Just as the body needs food frequently and consistently to stay healthy, relationships need the same nourishment as well. The closer the relationship, the more frequent and consistent the deposits need to be.

EMOTIONAL BANK ACCOUNT EVALUATION

Name of person: _____

Examine your balance with this person by evaluating deposits and withdrawals you have made. Mark deposits with a (+) and withdrawals with a (–). For each withdrawal, record changes you can make in the future to build deposits or repair trust.

Deposits and Withdrawals	(+) (–)	Changes I Can Make to Build Deposits or Repair Trust
Showing kindness and courtesy		
Keeping my promises		
Honoring expectations		
Showing loyalty when he/she is absent		
Apologizing when needed		

Name of person: _____

Deposits and Withdrawals	(+) (–)	Changes I Can Make to Build Deposits or Repair Trust
Showing kindness and courtesy		
Keeping my promises		
Honoring expectations		
Showing loyalty when he/she is absent		
Apologizing when needed		

➣ Key 2:

Deposits do not occur until the recipient considers it a deposit.

You simply don't know what constitutes a deposit until you understand the other person. For some, receiving feedback and comments on things they've done is a deposit. For others, it's a withdrawal. If your motives for making a deposit are not sincere, others will feel manipulated. It's not about doing or saying things that look positive. Your intentions can be good, but only the person you are interacting with can decide whether your gesture is a deposit or a withdrawal.

ARE YOU IN THE RED WITH RELATIONSHIPS?

It's time for an Emotional Bank Account evaluation. Choose two relationships you would like to improve and use the tool shown on the preceding page to determine whether you have a positive or negative trust balance with those people.

Use the Emotional Bank Account Log on the following pages to record your actions and words with each person over the next week.

Remember: This is not a scorecard, only a method to help you gain an awareness of your deposits and withdrawals.

EMOTIONAL BANK ACCOUNT LOG

Person: _____ Date: _____

Action	Deposit (+)	Withdrawal (–)

On a scale of –10 to +10, mark where you think you fall in terms of an Emotional Bank Account Balance with this person.

–10	0	+10

Describe three things you think this person would consider deposits, and determine when you could make these deposits.

Possible Deposits (to make in the future)	Date

Describe three things you think this person would consider withdrawals.

Possible Withdrawals (to make in the future)	Date

EMOTIONAL BANK ACCOUNT LOG

Person: _____   Date: _____

Action	Deposit (+)	Withdrawal (–)

On a scale of –10 to +10, mark where you think you fall in terms of an Emotional Bank Account Balance with this person.

|
–10   0   +10

Describe three things you think this person would consider deposits, and determine when you could make these deposits.

Possible Deposits (to make in the future)	Date

Describe three things you think this person would consider withdrawals.

Possible Withdrawals (to make in the future)	Date

HABIT 4

THINK WIN-WIN®

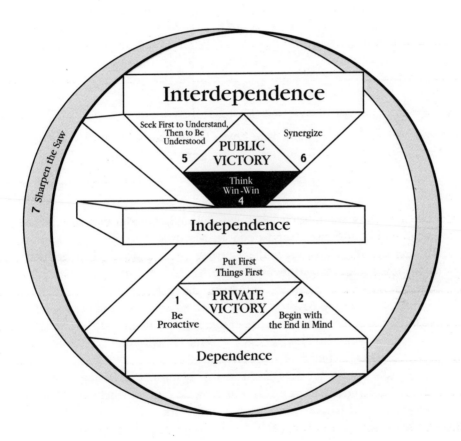

Before you begin this section of *The 7 Habits of Highly Effective People Personal Workbook*,
read pages 204–234 in *The 7 Habits of Highly Effective People*.

HABIT 4: THINK WIN-WIN

A person's true character is revealed by what he does when no one else is watching.
                                                            —UNKNOWN

IN ALL AREAS OF LIFE, effectiveness is largely achieved through the co-operative efforts of two or more people. Marriages and other partnerships are interdependent realities, and yet people often approach these relationships with an independent mentality, which is like trying to play golf with a tennis racket—the equipment isn't suited to the sport.

Most of us learn to base our self-worth on comparisons and competition. We think about succeeding in terms of someone else failing—that is, if I win, you lose; or if you win, I lose. Life is a zero-sum game. There is only so much pie, and if you get a big piece, there is less for me.

Win-Win sees life as a cooperative arena, not a competitive one. Win-Win is a frame of mind and heart that constantly seeks mutual benefit in all human interactions. Win-Win means agreements or solutions are mutually beneficial and satisfying.

Character is the foundation of Win-Win. A person or organization of any type that approaches conflicts with a Win-Win attitude possesses three character traits:

1. Integrity: conforming to your true feelings, values, and commitments.
2. Maturity: expressing your ideas and feelings with courage and consideration for the ideas and feelings of others.
3. Abundance Mentality: believing there is plenty for everyone.

DEVELOPING A WIN-WIN PARADIGM

Many people think in terms of either/or: either you're nice or you're tough. However, Win-Win requires that you be both. To go for Win-Win, you not only have to be empathic, you have to be confident. You not only have to be considerate and sensitive, you have to be brave. To do that—to achieve that balance between courage and consideration—is the essence of real maturity and is fundamental to Win-Win.

If you're high on courage and low on consideration, how will you think? Win-Lose. You'll be strong and ego-bound. You'll have the courage of your convictions, but you won't be very considerate of others. You'll borrow strength from your position and power, or from your credentials, your role, your seniority, or your affiliations.

If you're high on consideration and low on courage, you'll think Lose-Win. You'll be so considerate of others' feelings that you won't have the courage to express your own.

High courage and consideration are both essential to Win-Win. It's the balance of the two that is the mark of real maturity. If you have it, you can listen and you can empathically understand, but you can also courageously confront.

Choose two of your most important relationships for an evaluation of your ability to apply the Win-Win approach. Evaluate each relationship on your balance between courage and consideration. For example, if you consider yourself low on courage but high on consideration, place an X in the corresponding quadrant, and so on.

Now determine if you are out of balance in either of the relationships. Consider the elements of a Win-Win character: maturity and courage balanced with consideration and integrity. Next, decide what you might do to improve the situation and record your decision in the "Action needed" spaces below.

Relationship 1: _____

_____

Balance in relationship: _____

_____

_____

Action needed: _____

_____

_____

	Low → High CONSIDERATION
Win-Lose	Win-Win
Lose-Lose	Lose-Win

COURAGE (High ↑ Low)

Relationship 2: _____

_____

Balance in relationship: _____

_____

_____

Action needed: _____

_____

_____

_____

	Win-Lose	Win-Win
	Lose-Lose	Lose-Win

COURAGE — Low to High (vertical axis)

CONSIDERATION
Low ——————————→ High

CHANGING PLACES

From the previous exercise, select one relationship for which you want to develop a Win-Win Agreement, and follow these steps:

Put yourself in the other person's place and write down explicitly how you think that person understands the situation.

_____

_____

_____

_____

_____

From your own perspective, write the result that would constitute a win
for you.

_____

_____

_____

_____

_____

Approach the other person and ask if he or she would be willing to communicate until you both reach a point of agreement and a mutually beneficial
solution.

KEY POINTS IN DEVELOPING WIN-WIN RELATIONSHIPS

- Win-Win cultivates an Abundance Mentality: "We can find options that will be acceptable for everyone. There is always enough for everyone."
- Win-Lose cultivates a Scarcity Mentality: "My way is the only acceptable way. There's only so much, so I'd better get mine first."
- A Win-Win approach embodies courage to create an outcome that results in a win for you and for others. You must be willing to be completely honest and frank. Tell the other person precisely how you see the situation. Be willing to listen and to respect the other person's point of view.
- A Win-Win outcome requires trust. When you work for a Win-Win outcome, you seek mutual benefit.
- You can bring the Win-Win attitude to the table.
- Teams flourish when you have a Win-Win attitude because Win-Win cultivates interdependent relationships.
- When you use a Win-Win approach, you are not always nice, nor is it a manipulation technique.
- A Win-Win outcome is not always possible.

People who engage in Win-Win relationships do the following:

- Look for the good in other people.
- Communicate clear expectations.

- Seek others' ideas and listen with empathy.
- Are accurate, timely, and honest in communication.
- Treat people with respect and respond to the needs of others.
- Focus on the positive, but provide constructive feedback on improvement areas.

WIN-WIN
OPPORTUNITY QUESTIONS

The questions below will help you get started toward setting up a Win-Win Agreement around a specific situation or relationship.

QUESTION	ANSWER
What important relationship or issue would you like to improve or resolve by using a Win-Win approach?	
Do you have an Abundance Mentality (everyone can win) or a Scarcity Mentality (you must win)?	
What do you think will happen if you allow yourself to act in a Win-Lose manner?	
What do you think will happen if you approach this relationship or issue with a Win-Win attitude? What benefits can you foresee?	
What will you do to ensure that you reap the benefits of using a Win-Win approach?	
When will you take these actions?	

THE WIN-WIN AGREEMENT

A Win-Win Agreement is an effective tool for establishing the Win-Win foundation necessary for long-term effectiveness. It may be created between any two people who need to interact to accomplish desired results. In a Win-Win Agreement, the following five elements are made explicit:

- Desired results: What does your final outcome look like?
- Guidelines: What are the ground rules, the "shoulds" and "should nots"?
- Resources: What is it going to take? What resources are available?
- Accountability: Who will do what by when?
- Consequences: What happens when we are finished?

Refer to Stephen R. Covey's story beginning at the bottom of page 174 in *The 7 Habits of Highly Effective People*. In the space below, determine where the five elements of their Win-Win agreement occur.

Desired results:

_____

_____

_____

_____

_____

Guidelines:

_____

_____

_____

_____

Resources:

_____

_____

_____

_____

_____

Accountability:

_____

_____

_____

_____

_____

Consequences:

_____

_____

_____

_____

_____

Desired results: "Look, son," I said. "See how our neighbor's yard is green
    and clean?"
Resources: "I'd turn on the sprinklers."
Guidelines: "Now let's talk about 'clean,' son."

Accountability: "That's right. Twice a week . . ."
Consequences: So I did.

TAKING THE NEXT STEP

Make a commitment to practice a Win-Win approach in a specific area of your life. Use the table below to get started, or customize one to suit your needs.

QUESTION	ANSWER
What important relationship or issue would you like to improve or resolve by using a Win-Win approach?	
Do you have an Abundance Mentality (everyone can win) or a Scarcity Mentality (you must win)?	
What do you think will happen if you allow yourself to act in a Win-Lose manner?	
What do you think will happen if you approach this relationship or issue with a Win-Win attitude? What benefits can you foresee?	
What will you do to ensure that you reap the benefits of using a Win-Win approach?	
When will you take these actions?	

Now that you've determined the nature of your Win-Win, work through the elements in the table below to put your plan into action. Use the first column to check off each element as it is completed.

WIN-WIN AGREEMENT CHECKLIST		
	DESIRED RESULTS	Is the outcome defined? Does everyone involved envision the same outcome? Is it mutually beneficial?
	GUIDELINES	Have I identified any rules, policies, or specifications that I should follow?
	RESOURCES	Have I identified the necessary human, financial, and technical resources? Are they available?
	ACCOUNTABILITY	Have I identified what will be reported, and when and to whom it will be reported?
	CONSEQUENCES	Have I identified consequences for both failure and achievement? Are the consequences linked to desired results?

WIN-WIN AGREEMENT CHECKLIST		
	DESIRED RESULTS	Is the outcome defined? Does everyone involved envision the same outcome? Is it mutually beneficial?
	GUIDELINES	Have I identified any rules, policies, or specifications that I should follow?
	RESOURCES	Have I identified the necessary human, financial, and technical resources? Are they available?
	ACCOUNTABILITY	Have I identified what will be reported, and when and to whom it will be reported?
	CONSEQUENCES	Have I identified consequences for both failure and achievement? Are the consequences linked to desired results?

People who continually practice a Win-Win approach cultivate high-trust relationships. Why? Because they are treating others as they would like to be treated. Use the following checklist to see how you are doing with your relationships. Check the items you do more than 90 percent of the time.

	Your actions are consistent with your promises, values, and emotions. (You do what you say you will do—integrity.)
	You express your ideas and feelings with courage and consideration for the ideas and feelings of others.
	You believe there is plenty for everyone. You have an Abundance Mentality.
	You believe that people are doing their very best and that they deserve respect, consideration, and kindness.
	You listen intently to other people's position and seek to understand their position, behavior, and decisions. You disclose your position, explain your behavior, and validate your decisions.
	You communicate clear expectations.
	You focus on the positive but provide constructive feedback on potential improvement areas.

As you work on your Win-Win attitude, you will discover a remarkable thing: personal relationships will become easier! You will find that you are less territorial and dogmatic. When you have confidence in your own abilities and believe that there is enough for everyone, you are less fixated on getting your way all the time.

What do we live for, if not to make life less difficult for each other?
—*GEORGE ELIOT*

HABIT 5

SEEK FIRST TO UNDERSTAND, THEN TO BE UNDERSTOOD

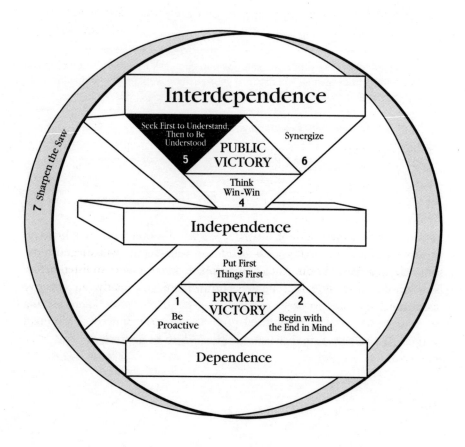

Before you begin this section of *The 7 Habits of Highly Effective People Personal Workbook*, read pages 236–259 in *The 7 Habits of Highly Effective People*.

HABIT 5: SEEK FIRST
TO UNDERSTAND, THEN
TO BE UNDERSTOOD

Although the tongue weighs very little, few people are able to hold it.
—*UNKNOWN*

COMMUNICATION IS the most important skill in life. Consider this: You've spent years learning how to read and write, and years learning how to speak. But what about listening? What training have you had that enables you to listen so you really, deeply understand another human being from that individual's frame of reference?

Seek first to understand, or Diagnose Before You Prescribe™, is a correct principle manifest in many areas of life. A wise doctor will diagnose before writing a prescription. The compassionate parent pauses to listen before handing out discipline that may be unwarranted. Similarly, an effective communicator will first seek to understand another's views before seeking to be understood. Next to physical survival, the greatest need of a human being is psychological survival—to be affirmed, to be appreciated, and to be understood.

HEY, ARE YOU LISTENING?

On a scale of 1 to 4, how do you think the following people would rate your listening skills?

	LOW			HIGH
Your best friend	1	2	3	4
Your partner	1	2	3	4
A close family member	1	2	3	4
A team member at work	1	2	3	4
Your boss	1	2	3	4

If you're like most people, you probably seek first to be understood. It's just part of human nature—you want to get your point across. And in doing so, you may *ignore* the other person completely, *pretend* you're listening, *selectively* hear only certain parts of the conversation, or *attentively* focus on only the words being said but miss the meaning entirely. So why does this happen? Well, because most people listen with the intent to reply and not to understand. You listen to *yourself* as you prepare in your mind what you are going to say, the questions you are going to ask, etc. One of the main reasons for this is that you filter everything you hear through your own auto-biography—*your* life experiences, *your* frame of reference. You check what you hear against your autobiography and see how it measures up. And consequently, you decide prematurely what the other person means before he or she finishes communicating. Do any of the following sound familiar?

"Oh, I know just how you feel. I felt the same way."
"I had that same thing happen to me."
"Let me tell you what I did in a similar situation."

Think of a time when someone didn't listen to you before prescribing an answer. How did you feel?

_____

_____

_____

_____

_____

When do you most often fail to listen to others? Why?

_____

_____

_____

_____

_____

AUTOBIOGRAPHICAL RESPONSES—
IT'S ALL ABOUT YOU

You might be saying, "Hey, now, wait a minute. I'm just trying to relate to the person by drawing on my own experiences. Is that so bad?" You may have very sincere desires, but true listening means that you forget about yourself and concentrate all your energies on being with the other person in real time. This is called *empathic listening,* and we'll talk more about it later. Now, be patient. We're trying to help you with a paradigm shift here! Because you so often listen autobiographically, you tend to respond in one of four ways:

Evaluate: You either agree or disagree.

Probe: You ask questions from your own frame of reference

Advise: You give counsel and solutions to problems based on your own experiences.

Interpret: You try to figure people out—explain their motives and behavior—based on your own motives and behavior.

The following example shows how four different friends respond to Joyce's statement about an idea she had for a family vacation. Circle the autobiographical response that is best represented in each conversation*:

Joyce: My family didn't like my idea for our vacation.
Carlos: Next time, if I were you, I'd talk to Beth about it first. She always seems to know the best thing to do.

Evaluate   Probe   Advise   Interpret

Joyce: My family didn't like my idea for our vacation.
Mitch: I'm sure the only reason they didn't like it was because it was going to cost way too much. Don't take it so personally.

Evaluate   Probe   Advise   Interpret

Joyce: My family didn't like my idea for our vacation.
Kaila: Did you let your husband know about your idea before you told everyone?

Evaluate   Probe   Advise   Interpret

Joyce: My family didn't like my idea for our vacation.
Melanie: Yeah, that can happen if you don't spend much time thinking about it first.

Evaluate   Probe   Advise   Interpret

People are so deeply scripted in these types of responses that they don't even realize when they use them. Now, we don't want you to think that autobiographical responses are always bad. When you use them at the right time with the right intent, they can be productive. But usually autobiographical responses force your opinion on others and sometimes you may be perceived as intrusive or unwilling to understand. Even if your intention is to help, giving advice or evaluating without being asked can backfire in the long run.

* Answers: Carlos—Advising; Mitch—Interpreting; Kaila—Probing; Melanie—Evaluating.

Do you have a relationship that needs improvement because you are listening autobiographically? Use the following tool to determine this:

INDIVIDUAL: _____	
Statement	Autobiographical Response

AUTOBIOGRAPHICAL RESPONSES— HOW DO I LISTEN?

Choose one relationship that you find challenging. During the week, listen, then write your responses from conversations you have with this person. Determine whether your responses are advising, probing, interpreting, or evaluating.

At the end of the week, review your notes. How might you change your listening next time? What would you do differently?

_____

_____

_____

_____

_____

EMPATHIC LISTENING—YOU HAVE THE RIGHT TO REMAIN SILENT

Genuine listening means suspending memory, desire, and judgment—and for a few moments, at least, existing for the other person.

—MICHAEL P. NICHOLS

EMPATHIC LISTENING	WITHIN THE OTHER'S FRAME OF REFERENCE
Attentive Listening **Selective Listening** **Pretend Listening** **Ignoring**	**Within one's own frame of reference**

As you can see from the diagram above, the highest form of listening is called empathic listening. Empathy is not sympathy. Sympathy is a form of agreement, a form of judgment. And it is sometimes the more appropriate emotion or response. But people often feed on sympathy. It makes them dependent. Empathic listening gets you inside another person's frame of reference. You look out through it, you see the world the way he or she sees it, and you understand how he or she feels. This does not necessarily mean you agree; it's that you fully, deeply, understand that person emotionally as well as intellectually. You temporarily let go of your perspective to understand his or her perspective.

Think of a time when someone made the effort to really understand you and your point of view. What was it this person said and did that made you feel understood?

_____

_____

_____

_____

_____

EARS, EYES, AND HEART

Empathic listening is not about just listening with your ears. It's about listening with your eyes and heart, too. When you and others speak, the meaning you communicate comes from three sources: the words you use, your body language, and how you say your words. Listening with your eyes means you pick up on nonverbal cues that another is communicating through his or her body language. Listening with your heart means you listen for feeling and meaning that is expressed through the tone and inflection of another's voice. And listening with your ears is simply hearing the actual words that are being said. It's important to remember that more than 90 percent of what people communicate does not come through words but through nonverbal communication, such as tone of voice and body language. This is where the paradigm shift usually occurs for people.

Communication is not just about words. Empathic listening is so powerful because it gives you accurate data to work with. Instead of projecting your own autobiography and assuming thoughts, feelings, motives, and interpretation, you're dealing with the reality inside another person's head and heart. You're focused on receiving the deep communication from another human soul.

LISTENING EXERCISE

The next time you have an opportunity to observe people communicating, cover your ears for a few minutes and just watch their body language. "Listen" to their hand gestures, their stance, and their facial expressions. What emotions are people communicating that might not come across in words alone?

This week pick two people and "listen" to their body language as you listen to their words. What did you notice?

_____

_____

_____

_____

_____

Did their body language agree with their words?

_____

_____

_____

_____

_____

What did you do if it didn't?

_____

_____

_____

_____

_____

LISTENING SKILLS—
ENHANCING EMPATHIC LISTENING

In addition to listening with your ears, eyes, and heart, seeking to understand another individual requires implementing a few listening skills as well. Yet these skills are only the tip of the iceberg when it comes to empathic listening. What lies below the surface of these skills is a sincere, true desire to understand another human being. If empathic listening skills are not used with this intent, then they may be perceived as manipulative and become ineffective. Even if your skills are not strong, if you are sincerely listening to understand, that intent will be heard loud and clear. Here are three basic skills to use when listening empathically:

- *Rephrase content.*
- *Reflect feeling.*
- *Ask questions for better understanding.*

When you *rephrase content,* you put the meaning of what another person said into your own words. You are trying to see things as he or she does—trying to understand things from his or her frame of reference. You are thinking about the content of what is being said and not just about words only. Here's an example:

> Steve: This project is really getting the best of me. I don't know if I'm going to get it done before my son's birthday.
> Lillian: It sounds like you have some deadlines you are trying to meet.

When you *reflect feeling,* you are concentrating on the way the other person feels about what he or she is saying. This is where listening with the ears, eyes, and heart really comes into play. Here's an example:

> Steve: This project is really getting the best of me. I don't know if I can get it done by my son's birthday.
> Lillian: Steve, you seem a little worried.

The true effectiveness of empathic listening comes when you combine rephrasing the content with reflecting the feeling. Here's an example:

> Steve: This project is really getting the best of me. I don't know if I can get it done by my son's birthday.
> Lillian: It seems like you are worried about some deadlines you are trying to meet.

A discerning empathic listener can read what's happening down deep fast, and can show a level of understanding and acceptance that helps people feel safe to open up layer after layer until they get to that soft inner core where the problem really is. Along the way it is important to *ask questions for better understanding*. These are not probing questions, but questions that help clarify and reach mutual understanding. Here are some examples:

You're frustrated by your daughter's lack of respect. Is that right? It seems like you're pretty upset with Phil. Is that what's bothering you? Anything else?

10 STEPS TO BECOMING AN EMPATHIC LISTENER

1. Practice saying, "Take your time, I'm listening," and really mean it.
2. Set aside your own agenda.
3. Be available and receptive emotionally as well as through body language.
4. Try to appreciate the other person's point of view.
5. Listen without being in a hurry to take over.
6. Try to imagine yourself in the other's place; feel what the speaker feels.
7. Help draw out thought and feeling by asking questions.
8. Have the speaker elaborate for further understanding.
9. Say, "Let me make sure I understand," and then restate the issue.
10. Be sensitive to the speaker's feelings.

It's true that becoming an empathic listener takes time, but it doesn't take anywhere near as much time as it takes to back up and correct misunderstandings when you're already miles down the road, to redo, and to live with unexpressed and unsolved problems.

If you really seek to understand, without hypocrisy and without guile, there will be times when you will be literally stunned with the pure knowledge and understanding that will flow to you from another human being.
—*STEPHEN R. COVEY*

DEVELOPING A LISTENING AWARENESS

During this week, pick a conversation that you wish you could have over again.

Who was it with? _____

When was it? _____

What was the topic? _____

Why do you want to do it over? _____

What happened? _____

_____

_____

_____

What can you do specifically to improve your empathic listening in this relationship?

_____

_____

Write the conversation as you would like it to go using empathic listening.

_____

_____

_____

SEEK TO BE UNDERSTOOD

Knowing how to be understood is the other half of Habit 5 and is equally critical to your effectiveness. In order to have influence with other people, they must first feel that you understand them. And once they feel understood, they are open to hearing your ideas, your counsel, and your point of view.

CHARACTER COMMUNICATES

One of the keys to your influence and your effectiveness in communicating your message to others is your example and conduct. Your example flows naturally out of your character—the kind of person you truly are—and not who others say you are or who you may want others to think you are. Your character is constantly communicating to others who you are. Because of what your character communicates, people will either trust or distrust you and your efforts with them. The questions below will help you examine your own character:

What is it about me that allows others to trust me?

_____

_____

_____

_____

_____

What is it about me that causes people not to trust me?

_____

_____

_____

_____

_____

Is there any part of my behavior where I am running hot and cold? For example, are there times when I am critical of people and then in the next moment forgiving?

_____

_____

_____

_____

_____

Do my private actions square up with my public actions? If not, why? Where are the discrepancies?

_____

_____

_____

_____

_____

COMMUNICATING
EFFECTIVE MESSAGES

Although character is extremely important in seeking to be understood, there are some other key areas that will help you in communicating an effective message. Whether you are communicating in writing, over the phone, or face-to-face in presentations, you want others to understand your logic and you want to convince them of the validity of that logic. Effective messages incorporate the following two key concepts:

- An understanding of the listener's needs, interests, concerns, and priorities.
- The sender's own ideas communicated clearly and specifically.

So, an effective communicator always identifies his or her audience and its needs first. Let's take a look at an example. Joseph is a salesperson for a large produce company. Here are some possible ways he could begin his presentation:

> "I'm Joseph Velasquez from Fresh Foods. My presentation will cover the following six points . . ."

> "I'm Joseph Velasquez from Fresh Foods. Before I begin, let me make sure I've captured your priorities for our time together. Based on conversations I've had prior to this meeting, here's what I think you're after. . . . Did I miss anything?"

Which one sounds better to you? It's probably pretty obvious that the second approach is much more effective than the first. In the second approach, Joseph acknowledges that those in the audience have their own needs and goals. He has also spent some time with the participants prior to the meeting to make sure he understands them. In the first approach, Joseph is acknowledging only his own needs and agenda. Now let's see how Joseph could continue his presentation:

> "I'd like to cover the material I have in about twenty-five minutes and then open it up for questions."

> "My goal in this presentation is to show how Fresh Foods can meet your needs in the Latino market. I'd like to leave with a clear sense of your operational plans and a 'go or no-go' decision to move forward next quarter."

Which one sounds better to you? In the first approach, Joseph is not very clear or specific about what he wants to accomplish. It leaves the audience guessing what the real next steps are. The only thing he clearly communicated was his desire to just get through the presentation. In the second example, Joseph communicates clearly and specifically his ideas and goals.

When Joseph first takes time to understand his audience and its needs, his audience is now receptive to his message and has a clear understanding of what will be discussed.

EVALUATING YOUR COMMUNICATION

Think of a recent phone conversation, e-mail, or face-to-face discussion where you stated your needs first.

Who was it with? _____

When was it? _____

What was the topic? _____

_____

What happened? _____

_____

_____

How might the outcome have been different if you had first stated the needs of the other person first?

_____

_____

_____

Did you communicate your ideas and logic clearly and specifically? If not, write them down below.

_____

_____

_____

How might the outcome have been different had you clearly and specifically communicated your ideas?

_____

_____

_____

HABIT 6

SYNERGIZE

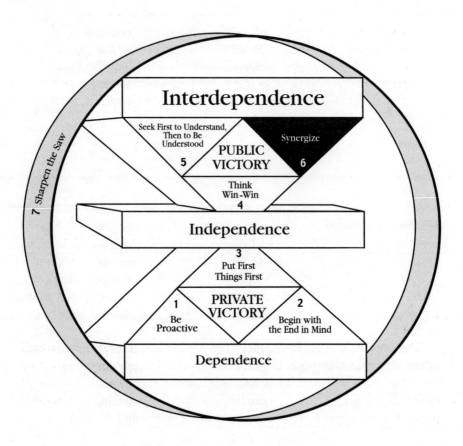

Before you begin this section of *The 7 Habits of Highly Effective People Personal Workbook*,
read pages 261–284 in *The 7 Habits of Highly Effective People.*

HABIT 6: SYNERGIZE

The essence of synergy is to value differences—to respect them, to build on strengths, to compensate for weaknesses. Once people have experienced real synergy, they are never quite the same again. They know the possibility of having other such mind-expanding adventures in the future.
                                                            —STEPHEN R. COVEY

HABIT 6: SYNERGIZE IS THE HABIT of creative cooperation. It is the essence of principle-centered leadership. Synergy is celebrating differences, teamwork, open-mindedness, and finding new and better ways together. It doesn't just happen, though. It's a process, and through that process you can create new alternatives—options that didn't exist before. Synergy is the idea that the whole is greater than the sum of its parts. One plus one equals three or more.

When people begin to interact together genuinely, and they're open to each other's influence, they begin to gain new insight. The capability of inventing new approaches, Third Alternatives, is increased exponentially because of differences. Synergy means you can literally produce something with another person that neither of you could have produced separately.

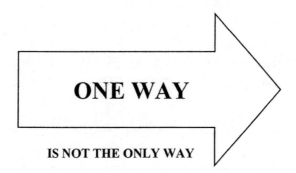

ONE WAY

IS NOT THE ONLY WAY

VALUING DIFFERENCES

Before you can leverage the strengths of others, you must first be able to recognize and value their differences. So, how much do you value differences? Take this short quiz.

Circle the number from 1 to 5 that most closely represents your normal behavior or attitude regarding the statement to the left. When you have answered all the questions, add up your total and check your score.

Scoring

41–50: Significantly leveraging the differences of others.
21–40: Moderately leveraging the differences of others.
10–20: Not taking advantage of the differences of others.

SYNERGY'S A-LIST

- *Have a healthy respect for diversity.* Everyone is unique and original, just like you.
- *Be able to relax around others.* Being wound too tight is for watches.
- *Value opinions whether you agree or not.* Leave "My Way" to Frank.
- *Create balance.* The idea is to give and take without being piggy about it.
- *Be responsive to new ideas.* No mind-closure allowed.
- *Develop trust.* Tough right out of the chute but worth it in the end.
- *Discover and share common interests.* Go out of your way to mind-meld often.
- *Humor.* Never leave home without it.
- *Don't stereotype.* You'll be wrong 100 percent of the time.
- *Be real.* Enough said.

	Never		Sometimes		Always
1. When I hear a point of view that is different from mine, I ask the person to elaborate on the idea.	1	2	3	4	5
2. When in disagreement, getting my ideas expressed is more important to me than following the opinion of the majority.	1	2	3	4	5
3. I frequently work with people who seem to have different perspectives from mine.	1	2	3	4	5
4. I try to use the knowledge and skills of others to better accomplish tasks.	1	2	3	4	5
5. I have found it very useful to have teams composed of people with different backgrounds.	1	2	3	4	5
6. I strongly believe that every person has a unique way of contributing to his or her family or group.	1	2	3	4	5
7. I actively seek to learn from others.	1	2	3	4	5
8. I share my opinions with others, even when our opinions seem to differ.	1	2	3	4	5
9. When working on a project, I seek out different ideas and opinions.	1	2	3	4	5
10. Whenever I am involved in a creative task, I tend to brainstorm with other people rather than rely on the opinions of experts.	1	2	3	4	5

PROFESSIONAL EXERCISE

....

Write down the name of a person you work with. In the area below, write the qualities this person possesses.

Talents/abilities (organized, knowledgeable, assertive, artistic, programmer, recruiter, writer, etc.)

_____

_____

_____

_____

_____

Background (education, race, gender, socioeconomic status, where he or she grew up, etc.)

_____

_____

_____

_____

Interpersonal skills (listener, communicator, speaker, teacher, mentor, role model, etc.)

_____

_____

_____

_____

_____

Character traits (sense of humor, micromanager, reliable, honest, diligent, opinionated, etc.)

_____

_____

_____

_____

_____

How different is this person from you?

_____

_____

_____

_____

_____

How could these differences contribute to accomplishing a common purpose?

_____

_____

_____

_____

IMPROVING RESULTS
BY VALUING DIFFERENCES

Differences are an opportunity, not an obstacle. The key is to remain open to hearing ideas so you can determine which ideas to combine to spark a better solution.

When faced with a difference of opinion, you can respond in several ways:

- **Attack.** You put down the idea. This is a defensive, fear-based response.
- **Tolerate.** You put up with but do not accept the idea.
- **Accept.** You accept that the idea is different, but you don't try to change anything.
- **Value.** You value the different idea and begin to see the opportunity in the new information.
- **Celebrate.** You seek out individuals who think differently, and you learn from those differences.

Think back to a gathering or conversation during which ideas were shut down, and answer the following questions:

1. When you first rejected the idea, what was it that turned you off? Was it the idea itself, the deliverer, or the way in which it was delivered? Did you dislike the idea because it wasn't yours?

_____

_____

_____

_____

2. What is your inner monologue saying? Is it saying, "That won't work," "You're nuts," or "We've never done it that way before"?

_____

_____

_____

_____

_____

3. If this was a work (team) situation, was there a "mob mentality" at work? Did the group quickly dismiss the idea because it didn't appear to support the group's typical way of thinking? If so, how?

_____

_____

_____

_____

_____

CAN YOU RELATE?

Answer the following questions true or false. Think about specific instances in your life before answering.

_____ I demand perfection from myself and everyone around me.

_____ I am surprised when others don't like me or my ideas.

_____ People continually make promises to me without following through.

_____ I don't have many friends whom I really like or trust.

_____ I get tired of all this political correctness. I don't have to like everyone.

_____ I don't appreciate other people's opinions of me.

_____ I don't like change.

_____ I work better alone than in groups.

_____ I tend to be more negative than positive.

_____ I'm afraid people will find out that I'm not what I appear to be.

If the majority of your answers are true, it's time to turn off the negativity tapes and rid yourself of your limited beliefs. In order to know yourself, you have to understand the lives and actions of others. Be a student of human nature and appreciate what everyone can bring to the party. If the majority of your answers are false, you're comfortable with yourself and how you relate to people of all kinds. You're a student of life and know learning from others helps you in your own life.

BREAKING DOWN THE BARRIERS

When you recognize the barriers to synergy, how do you break them down? You create an environment in which synergy can flourish. You use synergy producers. In the exercise below, assess how often you use synergy producers.

Circle the number from 1 to 5 that most closely represents how often you use synergy producers. When you have answered all the questions, add up your total and check your score.

	NEVER		SOMETIMES		ALWAYS
1. I challenge and question others.	1	2	3	4	5
2. I'm honest and candid in my communication.	1	2	3	4	5
3. I keep commitments.	1	2	3	4	5
4. I keep my cool in stressful situations.	1	2	3	4	5
5. I convey my feelings clearly.	1	2	3	4	5
6. I'm realistic in my expectations of others.	1	2	3	4	5
7. I share credit and success with others.	1	2	3	4	5
8. I value differences of opinion and truly seek to understand them.	1	2	3	4	5

	NEVER		SOMETIMES		ALWAYS
9. I discuss the facts without exaggerating.	1	2	3	4	5
10. I accept responsibility when things go wrong.	1	2	3	4	5

Scoring

45–55: Great job! You're a top synergy producer.
23–44: You're on the right track. Keep producing.
11–22: Watch yourself. You're blocking synergy.

CREATE THE THIRD ALTERNATIVE

Once you've bought into the idea that differences are strengths and not weaknesses, you're ready to find the "high way," or the Third Alternative, and create something better than what currently exists.

The Third Alternative is achieved when two or more people work together to create a better solution than those individuals could create separately. It's 1+1=3 or more. It's not your way or my way but a better way, a higher way.

There are five steps to a Third Alternative:

1. Define the problem or opportunity.
2. Listen to the other person.
3. Share your views.
4. Brainstorm options together.
5. Find the best solution together.

Choose a relationship or issue where you would like to work toward a more synergistic end. In the spaces below, work through the five steps to a Third Alternative.

1. Define the problem or opportunity.

_____

_____

_____

_____

_____

2. Listen to the other person.

_____

_____

_____

_____

_____

3. Share your views.

_____

_____

_____

_____

_____

4. Brainstorm options together.

_____

_____

_____

_____

_____

5. Find the best solution together.

_____

_____

_____

_____

_____

After you've worked toward a more synergistic end with the above situation, take a few minutes and write down in what ways this approach was different from how you would have handled it in the past. How did the new approach feel? Was it difficult for you? What steps will you take to ensure that you will continue to use this approach in the future?

_____

_____

_____

_____

_____

GET OVER IT! (YOUR BLOCKS TO SYNERGY, THAT IS)

In your life, have you found that there are people who drive you nuts or irritate you? Who are they? What do they do that irritates you?

Who   **What**

_____   _____

_____   _____

_____   _____

Look at each of the things you found irritating. What kinds of issues are they? Character issues (lack of integrity or discipline)? Competence issues (unable to do the job)? Cultural issues? Personality issues? Personal pet peeves? Now determine where you have direct control, indirect control, or no control.

Choose one issue from each area. How can you affect the synergy for each situation?

Direct Control:

_____

_____

_____

Indirect Control:

_____

_____

_____

No Control:

_____

_____

_____

Everything that irritates us about others can lead to an understanding of ourselves. People who upset us the most are often our best teachers! When you understand and are comfortable with yourself, it becomes easier to open yourself to the ideas of others. Always put yourself in the other person's shoes. Many of the "truths" you cling to are simply a result of one point of view—yours.

Coming together is a beginning; **keeping together** is progress; **working together** is success.

HABIT 7

SHARPEN THE SAW

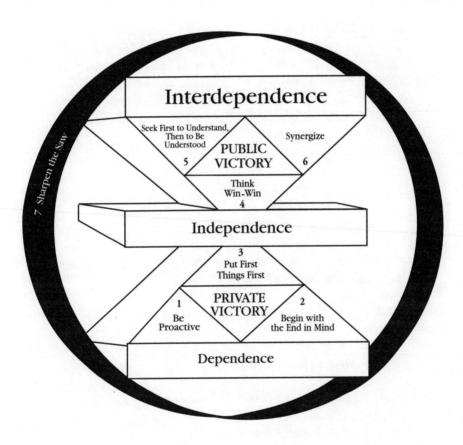

Before you begin this section of *The 7 Habits of Highly Effective People Personal Workbook,*
read pages 285–307 in *The 7 Habits of Highly Effective People.*

HABIT 7: SHARPEN THE SAW

Habit 7 is taking time to sharpen the saw. It's preserving and enhancing the greatest asset you have—you. It's renewing the four dimensions of your nature—physical, spiritual, mental, and social/emotional. This is the single most powerful investment we can ever make in life—investment in ourselves, in the only instrument we have with which to deal with life and to contribute.   —STEPHEN R. COVEY

HABIT 7: Sharpen the Saw is about balanced renewal in all four dimensions of human need: physical, spiritual, mental, and social/emotional. As you renew yourself in each of the four areas, you create growth and change in your life. You increase your capacity to produce and handle the challenges around you. When you don't renew yourself, you limit or even reverse your growth, and limit or decrease your capacity to produce and your ability to handle challenges.

So, you're thinking you don't have time to Sharpen the Saw? How can sharpening the saw increase capacity? Think about it.

- Time to cut a log with a dull saw—30 minutes.
- Time to sharpen the saw—5 minutes.
- Time to cut the log with a sharp saw—10 minutes.

Ka-ching! You just saved yourself fifteen minutes. You've never cut a log? How does this apply to you?

- Time left until your deadline and you're exhausted—5 hours.
- Time to Sharpen the Saw, refocus, and feel ready to go—30 minutes.
- Time it takes to finish the project when you're refreshed—4 hours.

Ka-ching! You just saved yourself thirty minutes. That's how it applies to you.

Feeling good doesn't just happen. You can't just snap your fingers and decide to feel good without making a conscious effort. Living a life in balance means taking the necessary time to renew yourself. It's all up to you. You can renew yourself through relaxation. Or you can totally burn yourself out by overdoing everything. You can pamper yourself mentally and spiritually. Or you can go through life oblivious of your well-being. You can experience vibrant energy. Or you can procrastinate and miss out on the benefits of good health. You can revitalize yourself in order to face a new day in peace and harmony. Or you can wake up in the morning full of apathy because your get-up-and-go has got-up-and-gone. Just remember that every day provides a new opportunity for renewal—a new opportunity to recharge yourself instead of hitting the wall. All it takes is the desire, knowledge, and skill.

GETTING READY

In order to reach a place of prosperity, you must engage in a process of renewal and revival. In order to maintain meaningful and consistent progress, you must be able to sense congruity or disparity.

The human endowment of conscience is called being self-aware. When you become self-aware, you can hear the intimations of conscience. Listen to your conscience. It can help you connect your conduct with your personal purpose.

Let your conscience guide you as you work through the next four pages of checklists. Being self-aware will help provide an assurance that the renewal plan you come up with in this section will be right for you.

Physical Checklist

Check only the items to which you can truthfully answer yes.

_____ I stay informed and current on both health and fitness information.

_____ I exercise twenty to thirty minutes at least three times a week.

_____ I am fully aware of my need for vitamins and minerals.

_____ I increase or maintain a strength program.

_____ I include cardiovascular and flexibility activities in my exercises.

_____ I get the proper amount of sleep.

_____ I rest or relax when my body needs it.

_____ I eat junk food less than twice a week.

_____ I have an effective, positive way of dealing with stress.

_____ I center my diet on a researched plan that fits my needs and goals.

Spiritual Checklist

Check only the items to which you can truthfully answer yes.

_____ I have defined what my values are, and I plan and live my life accordingly.

_____ I have created my mission statement. I rely on it to give vision to my purpose in life.

_____ I find daily renewal through meditation, prayer, study, or reflection.

_____ I frequently spend time in a place where I find spiritual renewal, e.g., in nature, a synagogue, a chapel, a temple.

_____ I live with integrity and honor.

_____ I keep my heart open to the truth.

_____ I am able to take a stand or tell the truth, even when opposed by others.

_____ I frequently serve others with no expectations of any type of returned favor.

_____ I can identify which things in life I can change and which things I cannot. I let go of the things I cannot change.

_____ I can connect to my inspirational guide as needed.

Mental Checklist

Check only the items to which you can truthfully answer yes.

_____ I read books and other publications regularly.

_____ I keep a journal or some sort of log, or engage in a regular writing process.

_____ I allow music, silence, or some sort of relaxation exercise to clear my mind on a daily basis.

_____ I challenge my mind through puzzles, problem solving, or games.

_____ I have a hobby.

_____ I continue my education either formally or informally.

_____ I engage in meaningful dialogue at least once a week.

_____ I visualize projects and plans so I have the end result in mind to guide the process.

_____ I have a system to retrieve information when I need it.

_____ I use a system to plan and organize my time and efforts.

Social/Emotional Checklist

Check only the items to which you can truthfully answer yes.

_____ I am reliable and dependable.

_____ I have a hopeful outlook on life.

_____ I am trusting and supportive of people in my Circle of Influence.

_____ I listen to others and hear what they have to say rather than thinking of what I want to say.

_____ I reach out to others and am empathic.

_____ I maintain my most important relationships.

_____ I sincerely apologize when I need to.

_____ I can persevere through the "hard times."

_____ I am aware of what it means to take good care of myself.

_____ I can control my impulses—cool down and act rather than react to people and situations.

Hopefully, the previous checklists have helped jumpstart your thinking for your personal renewal plan. Do you see areas where you are already doing well? How about areas where you could use some help? There is no right or wrong plan when it comes to renewal activities. You have to make it work for you.

Now that you've completed the checklists, take some time to think about the following questions. They will also get you thinking about where you might be out of balance, how to get your life in balance, and ultimately how to feel more rejuvenated. Jot down your thoughts and responses in the space provided.

1. If you could choose five things to do that would nourish your soul, what would they be?

_____

_____

_____

_____

_____

2. What makes those five things nourishing to you?

_____

_____

_____

_____

_____

3. What is cluttering your life?

_____

_____

_____

_____

_____

4. What keeps you awake at night?

_____

_____

_____

_____

5. What did you enjoy doing as a child?

_____

_____

_____

_____

_____

6. Remember a time when you were truly happy. What did it feel like? How can you feel that way again?

_____

_____

_____

_____

_____

7. How can you strengthen your relationship with a significant other?

_____

_____

_____

_____

_____

8. What inspires you?

_____

_____

_____

_____

_____

9. What memories can you pass on to your children about your ancestors?

_____

_____

_____

_____

_____

10. What are you doing so that your family remembers you?

_____

_____

_____

_____

_____

11. When was the last time you really checked in with yourself?

_____

_____

_____

_____

_____

12. What would ignite the childlike sense of wonder you once had?

_____

_____

_____

_____

_____

13. If you could build your very own retreat, what would it look like? How would you use it?

_____

_____

_____

_____

_____

14. What can you do less of?

_____

_____

_____

_____

_____

15. What do you want to do more of?

_____

_____

_____

_____

_____

16. What is complicating your life right now?

_____

_____

_____

_____

_____

17. How can you simplify it?

_____

_____

_____

_____

_____

18. Are you saying yes when you really want to say no? To what? To whom?

_____

_____

_____

_____

_____

Now that you've spent some time getting a better picture of where you are and where you want to be when it comes to Sharpening the Saw, let's break things down into more manageable pieces.

PLANNING

If you want a quality life, you have to plan and work for the results. Careful, consistent planning and action can provide renewal.

Planning is merely drawing a blueprint for the nurturing you wish to experience. There are two keys to successful planning: careful reflection, and giving the plan priority time. Careful reflection will assist you in determining which activities will sincerely regenerate your energies. Safeguarding time for your plan will securely keep it a priority in your daily and weekly schedule.

Exercising a plan that enriches all areas of your life will require about an hour a day. It is completely within your control. Keep in mind that it is very possible to combine activities from two or more of the dimensions. You may renew a relationship while walking together. Or why not attend a class on an interest you share with a friend? There are many ways to make your plan fit you and your lifestyle perfectly.

Renewal is a gift you give yourself, not an imposition. Give yourself time to get one area of renewal up, running, and fully launched. After executing it over a period of time, evaluate your progress. Assess your plan and see if it is fulfilling your needs. If your plan requires adjustment, then do it! It's not carved in stone. Move to the next aspect of your program once you are comfortable with the one you've been working on.

Plan, execute, and evaluate one step at a time. If you begin to feel overwhelmed, take a break and figure out what needs to be adjusted. This is about decreasing stress and increasing your feelings of renewal and balance, not the opposite!

PHYSICAL RENEWAL

Your body will honor you with wellness if you honor it with awareness.
—*ANONYMOUS*

IN ORDER FOR YOU to achieve physical renewal, you might need to go beyond your conventional notions of fitness and diet. If you're struggling for ideas, refer back to your checklist on pages 131 and 132. Would one of the unchecked items be a good place to start?

Take a few minutes to answer the following questions.

1. What does your body need for renewal?

_____

_____

_____

_____

_____

2. Is there some activity you've seen other people doing that you'd like to try?

_____

_____

_____

_____

_____

3. Do you want to learn more about nutrition?

_____

_____

_____

_____

_____

4. Do you want to learn more about fitness?

_____

_____

_____

_____

_____

Make a list of activities you think would enhance the physical dimension of your life and bring renewal. List things you are sincerely interested in. Putting down "go to the gym" when you know you hate it and won't do it isn't going to move you forward! List activities you would enjoy. You won't make progress by wearing yourself down. You are seeking to enliven potential, not beat it to death!

List your ideas for physical renewal activities:

_____

_____

_____

_____

_____

PLAN

Choose one activity from your list that really fits your current needs. Write it as an affirmation. For example, you might state your plan like this: "I will research my nutritional options for ten days."

I will _____

_____

Once you have clarity on which action to take, it's time to plan. In your Franklin Planning System, or other planning tool of choice, make an appointment with yourself to begin your activity.

If the activity is something such as exercising aerobically for thirty minutes three to four times a week, plan the exercise into adequate spots within a three- to four-week time frame. It's recommended that you see a medical doctor before increasing any physical activity.

If the activity is something like making changes in what you eat and drink, take the first few days or even the first week to do research. Before you make your plan, plan to learn what changes are right for you. Then spend the next few weeks implementing the changes in moderation as needed.

EVALUATE

At the end of the three- to four-week period, plan an evaluation session. Schedule it now. During this session, take stock in what worked and what didn't. Change what didn't work and replace it with something you feel will work for you. Use the space below to record your successes, as well as those things you need to change.

_____

_____

_____

_____

_____

Remember! Spoiling yourself once in a while is actually good for you. It triggers endorphins. It's satisfying. You don't have to throw down the self-discipline gauntlet, just relax a little. Indulging can help you control cravings so they don't turn into binge-fests. Balance is about enjoying bliss, not just cutting out the junk.

SPIRITUAL RENEWAL

The soul was never put in the body . . . to stand still.
—JOHN WEBSTER

SPIRITUAL RENEWAL is a dimension of personal leadership and direction. The direction comes from your moral compass. This is a private aspect of your renewal. Your mission—your purpose in life—is your inner compass. Your values are the mechanisms that point the way.

Honoring and nurturing your inner compass is a most important task. By charting a course of spiritual renewal, you provide a rekindling of the "fire within." This provides the energy necessary to travel the course your compass has charted.

IDENTIFY

Spiritual renewal encompasses many areas. It will be different for each person. Spiritual renewal is personal and can be extremely intimate. Interpreting what your frame of reference tells you about what is happening "out there" is spiritual renewal.

Record your thoughts and the answers to the following questions:

1. Which endeavors will stimulate and inspire you as well as tie you to what you value most?

_____

_____

_____

2. What types of things can you do and in what types of places can you
   spend your time so you are inspired and spiritually refreshed?

_____

_____

_____

_____

_____

3. How do you personally connect to a higher power?

_____

_____

_____

_____

_____

4. Do your actions align with your values?

_____

_____

_____

_____

_____

List the spiritually renewing ideas that you have thought of:

_____

_____

_____

_____

_____

PLAN

Which renewal idea from your list seems right for you at this time? Write it as an affirmation. For example, if you have determined to visit the mountains several times a month for spiritual regeneration, you might write, "I will visit the mountains four times this month on the following days . . ."

I will _____

_____

In your Franklin Planning System or other planning tool, schedule the times when you will follow through on your commitment.

EVALUATE

Determine a time, perhaps three to four weeks from now, when you can appraise your progress. How is it going? Do you feel a spiritual connection—a renewal—spreading throughout your life? If not, what adjustments can you make?

In the space below, record your successes and any changes you want to make to your plan.

_____

_____

_____

_____

_____

_____

_____

_____

_____

BEING SELF-AWARE

Remember reading about the aspect of "conscience"? Conscience is the endowment of being self-aware. It's a gift to know the inner callings of your purpose.

Being self-aware can assist you in taking your renewal activities to a level of maximum potential. When a person connects renewal with personal purpose, one's life becomes congruent with one's authentic nature. When this occurs, your fire within is alive and well. You might find yourself seeking the spontaneous transmission of renewing energy as a way of life—a way of being on a daily basis.

MENTAL RENEWAL

....

Education—continuing education, continually honing and expand-
ing the mind—is vital mental renewal. Sometimes that involves the
external discipline of the classroom for systematized study programs;
more often it does not. Proactive people can figure out many ways to
educate themselves. It is extremely valuable to train the mind to stand
apart and examine its own program. That, to me, is the definition of a
liberal education—the ability to examine the programs of life against
larger questions and purposes and other paradigms.
                                                    —STEPHEN R. COVEY

IN TODAY'S WORLD, if you don't keep yourself mentally sharp, you're in
big trouble. Mental stimulation comes from a wide variety of sources. It isn't
always about renewing credentials, although that is important. Fiction, art,
educational TV, puzzles, and games can be about stretching yourself mentally as well.

IDENTIFY

....

Researchers believe that vigorous mental exercise literally grows brain cir-
cuitry. Furthermore, the process does not diminish with age. If this is true,
exercising your mental capacities should keep you as young and vital as exercising your body can. Record your thoughts about and the answers to the
following questions:

1. Do you like solving some type of puzzle? What types?

_____

_____

_____

_____

_____

2. Have you tried to write your own poetry? What was it like?

_____

_____

_____

_____

_____

3. Would you like to learn how to do simple maintenance on your car or an appliance?

_____

_____

_____

_____

_____

4. Is there something you've always been curious about? What is it?

_____

_____

_____

_____

_____

5. Do you like to read or visit museums? What sorts of books? Which type of museum?

_____

_____

_____

_____

6. Is there a hobby or craft you'd like to take up? Which ones?

_____

_____

_____

_____

Now list your ideas for mental renewal activities:

_____

_____

_____

_____

_____

PLAN

Select the idea you want to start with. State your activity as an affirmation. For example, if your idea is to learn a new word each day, you might state it like this: "I will learn one new word each day for the next three weeks."

I will _____

_____

In your Franklin Planning System or other planning tool, schedule time for this activity. If you've decided to learn a new skill, you may need to schedule one or two time slots a week. Schedule your time across several weeks.

EVALUATE

Make an appointment with yourself for self-evaluation at the end of a month. Schedule it in your planning tool now. During your evaluation, check on how well your mental renewal plan is working. If necessary, change or tweak what needs to be adjusted. Record your progress below.

_____

_____

_____

_____

_____

_____

_____

_____

_____

SOCIAL/EMOTIONAL RENEWAL

The most important ingredient we put into any relationship is not what we say or do, but what we are.

—STEPHEN R. COVEY

RELATIONSHIPS CAN BE ONE of the most enriching elements of life. For each relationship the questions of trust, kindness, values, and loyalty come into play.

Often in our hurried world, we operate on the mistaken assumption that we can quickly accumulate friends and close colleagues. We often mistake acquaintances for relationships.

Meaningful relationships are not like the mold accumulating on the cheddar in your fridge. They require conscious effort. Don't forget, each relationship is like a bank account. The quality of the relationship depends on what you put into it. Keeping promises, being courteous and kind, offering support, listening, and taking time for the other person are just a few ways to make deposits.

Of course there are certain things that will make withdrawals, and you'll want to minimize those. Keep your Emotional Bank Accounts growing, and you'll see the dividends in deeper, more meaningful relationships.

Before you start charting out the activities you want to use in your plan for this human dimension, consider one concept. Consider social/emotional restoration as having two equally important branches: self and others.

SELF

Recognize that full renewal will never be achieved if you don't first invest in a personal Emotional Bank Account, or the branch known as "self."

We all need respect. We all experience areas of emptiness and need. These are places where unconditional love and regard are needed but are not always found. You don't have to go around feeling empty and worn. You can proactively take action. You are the primary person in charge of seeing that your needs are met. It begins with you.

Your first step in social/emotional renewal should be a step to care for yourself. What can you do that shows regard, care, and love for self?

_____

_____

_____

_____

_____

One man makes deposits in his own Emotional Bank Account by trusting his instincts. He reports that he doesn't always know why he does what he does, but he has learned to honor this sense of inner peace.

IDENTIFY

It is fully legitimate to nurture yourself before reaching out to others. You can't give someone a drink of water from an empty glass. Take time to fill your glass and you will see the Abundance Mentality replenishing your glass and spilling over into your other relationships. If you sincerely take good care of yourself, you'll gain genuine insight into how to care for others.

Jot down your answers to and thoughts on the following questions:

1. Do you have a quiet, safe place to retreat to?

_____

_____

_____

_____

_____

2. Do you surround yourself with sincerely supportive people?

_____

_____

_____

_____

3. Have you considered taking yourself out on a date?

_____

_____

_____

_____

4. Do you allow yourself to believe in your goals and dreams?

_____

_____

_____

_____

5. Do you know how to provide for your personal needs?

_____

_____

_____

_____

_____

Reflect on experiences or times when you felt cared for, accepted, needed, and loved. Can you provide a similar experience where you have provided service to others?

List your ideas for self-renewal. What can you do right now?

_____

_____

_____

_____

_____

PLAN

Which idea seems most immediate? Write it as an affirmation. For example, if you've determined that giving yourself a two-hour date each week would restore you, you might write it like this: "I will schedule two hours a week to take myself on a date."

I will _____

_____

In your Franklin Planning System or other planning tool, plan out the implementation of your idea. Schedule an evaluation date. Try making it sometime during the first two weeks of your plan.

EVALUATE

Plan to evaluate your personal renewal at the end of your first week. Schedule your evaluation day now. Take time to determine if you feel more refreshed and valued after having your plan in action.

If you are reaping your desired results, keep up the good work. If you need to adjust your plan, do so, and give yourself another week of experimenting to get the renewal you want.

In the space below, record those things that worked and those that didn't. What will you change to make it work for you?

_____

_____

_____

_____

_____

_____

_____

_____

_____

_____

OTHERS

As you continue to plan activities that cultivate a deep inner sense of your personal worth and security, you may start noticing that you have become involved in activities that grow out of an Abundance Mentality. This model is based on the recognition that there is plenty out there and enough to spare for everyone. This mentality takes the personal joy, satisfaction, and fulfillment you find in personal care, and starts to extend it outward.

Because you have started to recognize your own unlimited possibilities and have appreciation for your own uniqueness, you start to value more of these qualities in others. From this perspective, you appreciate the remarkable talents and inner direction of others. Often you begin to feel compelled to listen harder, communicate more clearly, and honor and respect others through positive interaction. You start making deposits into their Emotional Bank Accounts.

IDENTIFY

Each relationship requires a unique type of deposit. Some relationships equate hugs, compliments, and small gifts with deposits. For other relationships, dependability and pulling your own weight are the primary deposits. Think of several activities you could engage in that would enrich your relationships with others. Has someone asked for your time? Is there someone in your family or close circle of friends who needs and wants your attention? Is there someone you value and want to get to know better?

Answer the following questions:

1. How can you strengthen your relationship with a partner or spouse?

_____

_____

_____

_____

_____

2. Do you need to learn more about what types of deposits work for the other person involved in a relationship?

_____

_____

_____

_____

_____

3. Do you need to clear time for someone?

_____

_____

_____

_____

4. Do you need to help out at your children's school?

_____

_____

_____

_____

5. Do you need to be more respectful?

_____

_____

_____

_____

6. Do you need to learn to listen?

_____

_____

_____

_____

_____

List actions you are interested in taking in order to make social investments.

_____

_____

_____

_____

PLAN

Which idea do you want to start on right now? Write it as an affirmation. For example, if you have decided that you want to enliven your relationship with a child, you might have an affirmation statement that reads: "I will read with my child for 10 to 15 minutes each weeknight."

I will _____

_____

In your Franklin Planning System or other planning tool, plan your time over the next week to renew this relationship.

EVALUATE

People are living, breathing organisms. You would not leave a plant or animal uncared for over a long period of time. Internal human needs require just as much constant attention as external, physical needs. If you want social/emotional renewal, you will need to plan activities and their assessments more frequently to foster these relationships. Try assessing your success and progress after the first week.

If you're really brave, try asking for feedback. Check your progress from the perspective of those with whom you relate.

PART FOUR

SO WHAT NOW?

SO WHAT NOW?

Life is not orderly. No matter how hard we try to make life so, right in the middle of it we die, lose a leg, fall in love, drop a jar of applesauce.
—NATALIE GOLDBERG

IMPLEMENTING A RENEWAL PLAN can seem like a daunting thing. You've gone through all the steps in the previous pages and you might still feel bogged down, overwhelmed, and not renewed at all. That's not unusual. If you've been able to implement your plan to your satisfaction, congratulations to you! If not, read on. We've provided some hints, tips, ideas, and encouragement for you to use on your journey.

WHAT TO DO WHEN YOU'RE READY TO LOSE YOUR MIND

Get Some Oxygen.

Focused breathing can help you control your physical responses to stress. Put your tongue on the roof of your mouth behind your teeth, inhale deeply through your nose, and fill up with air until your stomach sticks out like a baby's. Then slowly release the air through your nose or mouth. Do this at least three times. It will help you loosen up and settle down.

Take a Perspective Check

Get the "big picture" quickly by asking yourself: "Okay, will I care about this in a month? In a year?" If you're going to freak out, make sure it's for a good reason. If your reason for stressing suddenly seems ridiculous, laugh it off.

Choose Your Response

Pick the appropriate and productive emotion: anger, courage, humor, compassion, sadness, or whatever. Any emotion is okay as long as you remain in control and handle the situation with a little finesse.

A SELF-RENEWAL PLAN

Start small. Start your plan with an activity that you feel very motivated doing. Never had the desire to take a class in metaphysics? So what? Find something you are truly interested in. There's got to be something!

Keep it going. Continue using any successful activity you're already doing for renewal. No need to reinvent the wheel!

Take your time. Play with different ideas and experiment until you find the right combination of things that work for you. Don't forget that you can combine activities from different dimensions and kill two birds with one stone!

Don't overwhelm yourself. If all of your renewal activities fill daily time slots, you could become overwhelmed rather than enlivened. Go easy on yourself and don't expect a quick fix.

Continually adjust. Very rarely will a plan work forever. Times change, your interests and abilities will change. Plan to continually adjust and update your activities.

Be self-aware. Your likes, dislikes, and personal style will help you in planning activities, which yield your greatest restorative potential.

YOUR OWN LITTLE SANCTUARY

Is your home a place of refuge or just a nagging reminder that carpets do indeed require regular vacuuming? Here are a few things you can do to make it a place you want to come home to.

Splurge on fresh flowers once in a while. They brighten your home and can smell wonderful. Even a bunch of daisies in a glass can create a sense of serenity.

Turn on some beautiful music. It can change your mood and help you wind down, relax, and regroup.

Have a clean-up bin. Pick up clutter and put it in a sort-through-later bin. A clean room can make your surroundings more peaceful.

Try some aromatherapy. It's not hard to get your hands on scented candles, oils, sachets, or sprays. A wonderful smell can be truly soothing.

Reap the benefits of live plants. Plants can help hydrate your skin, lower your blood pressure, and reduce dust and indoor chemical pollutants. They look nice, too!

FIVE STEPS TO INNER RENEWAL

Remember. Buried under the years and experiences of your life is a memory of a dream, a forgotten wanting, a simple whim. Capture the memory once again and make it a reality.

Create. Sometimes we are afraid to express ourselves in a way that leaves tangible evidence of our thoughts and feelings. Create something, even if you start by revisiting a box of crayons.

Absorb. Often what you have is what you've chosen to have. There must be something about your "now" that you can be fully glad is yours. Maybe it's a sunset, or a flower garden, or a favorite piece of music. Allow yourself to absorb one gift that's yours.

Want. If you never felt the discomfort of thirst, your body would dry up. The wanting inside of you should be honored like thirst. What is it? What do you want? Drink it up. Find a way to put the wanting at peace. Then listen for the next want. Quenching wants nurtures your soul.

Need. We often neglect our needs as much as we do our wants. A need is deeper than a want. If you need rest, take it. If you need laughter, create it. If you need love, grow it.

FOUR EASY WAYS
TO SIMPLIFY YOUR LIFE

Schedule some downtime every day. Write in a journal or take a quiet bath before bed. Recognize that not doing it all is okay—even important.

Make a plan to pay off credit card balances. Yes, you can do it. Ditch all the cards except two—one for business expenses and one for personal expenses. And *do* leave home without them whenever you can!

Leave the TV off one night a week. You'll be surprised at the extra time you have. Leaving it off may even become a habit!

Don't be a slave to the phone. Let your machine pick up—if it's important, they'll leave you a message. When you get annoying solicitation calls, ask to have your name removed from the company's list.

Be patient with yourself. Self-growth is tender; it's holy ground.
—*STEPHEN R. COVEY*

CONCLUSION

IMPLEMENTING THE 7 HABITS can help you take responsibility for your life, decide what's really important, and live by correct principles. In addition, it can help you develop an Abundance Mentality.

Breaking away from old habits to empower yourself to learn new habits can be compared to the space shuttle leaving the atmosphere. Most of the energy is spent breaking away from the gravity of the earth. An enormous seven million pounds of total thrust is required to lift the shuttle during its eight-and-a-half minute journey into the vacuum of space.

Having overcome earth's gravity and traveling 300 miles above the earth at a sobering 17,500 miles per hour, astronauts suddenly experience an endless range of new possibilities in their weightless environment. Former U.S. senator Jake Garn recalls, "I found that I could move myself backward just by blowing air, and that a fingertip push could propel me faster than I wanted to go."

Likewise, to overcome the gravity pull of deeply embedded habits, we must break free from environmental expectations and social definitions. Once we do that, we gain real power and freedom.

START LIVING
THE 7 HABITS

You must have a continual improvement process in your life if you hope to thrive and prosper in an environment of constant change and upheaval. Avoiding the conditions of mediocrity, stagnation, and complacency requires great initiative, vision, and discipline, and can occur only if you are willing to pay the price to achieve this Private Victory.

To start living the 7 Habits, consider the following steps:

1. Learn to be still, to meditate, and to live with some silence. Ponder your mission statement and unique human endowments. You should also start by making small commitments so you don't get overcommitted.
2. Continually Sharpen the Saw and spend time each day renewing the four dimensions of your life: physical, spiritual, mental, and social/emotional. As a part of this self-renewal process, at the beginning of each day, ask yourself the following questions, then think about your mission statement, what you stand for, and what your purpose is in life:

    - What is it that I want to do today?
    - How am I going to deal with my loved ones today?
    - How am I going to handle today's challenges?

3. Make deposits into the Emotional Bank Accounts of your key relationships, and nurture the people you are close to. Success and harmony at home precede all other successes.
4. Spend more time in Quadrant II. Decide what is really important and work on that. Say no to those things that are not in Quadrant II and work on empowering others to free up more of your own time and energy.
5. Make sure your mission statement is intact, and work on developing a family mission statement.
6. Take responsibility for deciding what your family is all about, then plan and execute according to your priorities.
7. Regularly review the 7 Habits and teach them to others, such as family members and work associates.
8. Be patient and kind to yourself in the process; however, realize that to make these habits and principles a part of your life, you must pay the price by actually living them, rather than merely understanding them intellectually.

[T]he harder the conflict, the more glorious the triumph. What we obtain too cheap, we esteem too lightly; it is dearness only that gives everything its value. . . . I love the man that can smile in trouble, that can gather strength from distress and grow brave by reflection. 'Tis the business of little minds to shrink; but he whose heart is firm, and whose conscience approves his conduct, will pursue his principles unto death. —THOMAS PAINE

Important Note

This publication is a personal workbook and is intended exclusively for individual use.

The workbook may not be reproduced or used in a classroom or other group setting, or used by organizations as part of a training programme.

Permission to use FranklinCovey materials with groups or organizations may be granted to specific organizations through a written licence, subject to conditions and upon payment of applicable licence fees. For information on becoming a licensed facilitator please call +44 (0) 1295 274100 if within the UK and Ireland, or your local office if elsewhere.

ABOUT FRANKLINCOVEY

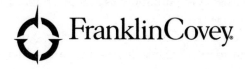

FRANKLINCOVEY IS A GLOBAL LEADER in effectiveness training, productivity tools and assessment services for organizations and individuals. We work in partnership with many of the world's foremost companies and public sector bodies, with one mission: to help improve the effectiveness and performance of their people and their enterprise, significantly and measurably.

We help people and organizations to deliver sustained superior performance by developing key attributes: individual effectiveness, enduring leadership capability, and the the ability to focus and execute on their highest priorities.

FranklinCovey's approach goes to the heart of success, both personal and business. Over the past 15 years the company has grown rapidly through a network of direct offices and licensed partners to become a global leader in its field. Now FranklinCovey has 39 offices covering more than 100 coutries, and facilitates learning for many thousands of people around the world every year.

Our core services include:

- *Workshops*: our corporate and public workshops include The 7 Habits of Highly Effective People, the 4 Roles of Leadership, FOCUS: Achieving Your Highest Priorities, and The 4 Disciplines of Execution.
- *Assessment tool and processes*: for example the xQ Survey and Debrief, whcih healps leaders assess their organization's 'execution quotient.'
- *Planning systems*: the FranklinCovey Planning system is used by many thousands of people to manage their lives. It comes in traditional paper format or as a range of software solutions to suit every style of working,

complementing desktops (including Outlook integration), Tablet PCs and handhelds.

To find out more about FranklinCovey:

- For the UK and Ireland, please contact the office below.
- If elsewhere in the world, please contact one of the local offices listed on the following pages or on our website.

FranklinCovey Europe Ltd
Grimsbury Manor
Grimsbury Green
Banbury
OX16 3JQ

Tel: +44 (0) 1295 274100
Fax: +44 (0) 1295 274101
e-mail: enquiries@franklincoveyeurope.com
web: www.franklincoveyeurope.com

Training and development:
Tel +44 (0) 870 870 7600

Product orders, enquiries and catalogues:
Tel: +44 (0) 870 870 7600

FranklinCovey Offices Worldwide

Europe/Middle East/Africa

Country	Office	Tel	Contact
Austria	FranklinCovey Austria	Tel: +49 ª0º 611 9777 4215	Email: www.franklincovey.at Web: info@franklincovey.at
Belgium & Luxemburg	FranklinCovey Belgium & Luxemburg	Tel: +32 11 80 12 58	Email: info@franklincovey.be Web: www.franklincovey.be
Czech Republic	FranklinCovey Czech and Slovacs	Tel: +420 261 099 341	Email: info@franklincovey.cz Web: www.franklincovey.cz
Egypt	Egyptian Leadership Training & Consultancy	Tel: +(202) 336 8911 or +(2010) 566 0149	Email: fc_eltc@sofiocom.com.eg Web: www.eltc.com.eg
France	FranklinCovey-Cegos	Tel: +33 1 55 00 90 90	Email: franklincovey.@cegos.com Web: www.cegos.com
Germany,	FranklinCovey GSA Focus	Tel: +49 611 9777 4215	Email: info@franklincovey.de Web: www.franklincovey.de
Greece	DMA Hellas Group	Tel: +30 210 698 5946	Email: info@franklincovey.gr Web: www.franklincovey.gr
Hungary	FCCoL Hungary Managament Consulting	Tel: +36 1 412 1884	Email: office@franklincovey.hu Web: www.franklincovey.hu
Ireland	FranklinCovey Europe Ltd	Tel: +353 1664 1706	Email: Ireland@franklincoveyeurope.com Web: www.franklincoveyeurope.com
Israel	Momentum Training Ltd.	Tel: +97 2 979 61055	Email: goz@mimentum.co.il
Italy	Cegos Italia S.p.A	Tel: +39 2 80672417	Email: roberto,monti@cegos.it Web: www.franklincovey.cegos.it
Lebanon	Starmanship & Associates	Tel: +961 1 393 494	Web: www.starmanship,com Email: starman@cyberia.net.lb
Netherlands	FranklinCovey Netherlands	Tel: +31 33 453 0627	Email: info@franklincovey.nl Web: www.franklincovey.nl
Nigeria	FReStraL Ltd	Tel: +2341 264 5885	Email: enquiries@restral.com Web: www.franklincoveynig.com
Nordic Region	FranklinCovey Nordic Approach	Tel: +45 70226612	Email: info@franklincovey.dk Web: www.franklincovey.dk
Poland, Estonia, Belarus, Ukraine, Moldova, Georgia, Azerbaijan, Armenia, Kazakhstan and Uzbekistan	FranklinCovey Central Eastern Europe	Tel: +48 22 824 11 28	Email: office@franklincovey.pl Web: www.franklincovey.pl
Portugal	Cegoc-Tea, Lda	Tel: +351 21 319 19 60	Email: info@franklincovey.pt Web: www.franklincovey.pt
Russia	FranklinCovey Russia	Tel: +7 095 787 8577	Email: sp@mti.ru
South Africa	FCSA Organisation Services (Pty) Ltd	Tel: +27 11 807 2929	Email: info@franklincovey.co.za Web: www.franklincovey.co.za
Spain	TEA-CEGOS, S.A.	Tel: +34 912 705 000	Email: franklincovey@tea-cegos.es Web: www.tea-cegos-franklincovey.com
Switzerland	Franklincovey Switzerland S	Tel: +49 611 9777 4215	Email: info@franklincovey.ch Web: www.franklincovey.ch
Turkey	ProVista Management Consulting Ltd.	Tel: +90 232 247 50 21	Email: info@franklincovey.com.tr Web: www.franklincovey.com.tr
UAE, Syria, Iraq, Jordan, Oman,	FranklinCovey – Qiyada Consultants	Tel: +971 4 332 2244	Web: www.franklincovey.com Email: info@franklincoveyme.com
Saudi Arabia	FranklinCovey – Qiyada Consultants	Tel: +971 966 1416 3328	Email: enquiries@qiyada.com.sa
UK	FranklinCovey Europe Ltd	Tel: +44 1295 274100	Email: enquiries@franklincoveyeurope.com Web: www.franklincoveyeurope.com

Americas

Argentina	LFCA S.A. Organizational Services	Tel: +5411 4372 5820	Email: info@franklincovey.com.ar Web: www.franklincovey.com.ar
Bermuda	Effective Leadership Bermuda	Tel: +441 236 0383	Email: franklincovey.bda@logic.bm
Brazil	FranklinCovey Brasil	Tel: +55 11 5105 4400	Email: info@franklincovey.com.br Web: www.franklincovey.com.br
Canada	FranklinCovey Canada	Tel: +519 740 2580	Email: generalinquiries@franklincovey.ca Web: www.franklincovey.ca
Canada (Quebec)	Big Knowledge Enterprises Inc.	Tel: +514 844 2300	Email; patrick.obrien@versalys.com Web: www.bigknowledge.com
Chile	FranklinCovey Chile	Tel: +56 2 4489658	
Colombia	FranklinCovey Colombia	Tel: +57 1 610 2736	Email: clccolom@colomsat.net.com
Costa Rica	FranklinCovey Costa Rica	Tel: +506 256 4242	Email: franklincoveycr@fcla.com
Ecuador	FranklinCovey Ecuador	Tel: +59 34 2850485	
El Salvador	FranklinCovey El Salvador	Tel: +503 263 3377	Email: franklincoveysv@fcla.com
Honduras	FranklinCovey Honduras	Tel: +504 552 1952	Email: msabillon@fcla.com Web: franklincoveyhn@fcla.com
Latin America	Advantage Management International, Inc.	Tel: +407 644 7117	Email: franklincovey@fcla.com Web: www.fcla.com
Mexico	FranklinCovey Mexico	Tel: +52 555 322 3800	Email: fcmex@franklincoveymex.com Web: www.franklincovey.com.mx
Nicaragua	FranklinCovey Nicaragua	Tel: +505 270 7864	Email: franklincoveyni@fcpma.com
Panama	Leadership Technologies, Inc.	Tel: +507 264 8899	Email: franklincovey@fcpma.com Web: www.fcla.com
Peru	FranklinCovey Perú	Tel: +51 1475 1000	Peru
Puerto Rico	FranklinCovey Puerto Rico	Tel: +787 977 9094	Email: franklincoveypr@fcla.com Web: www.fcla.com
Trinidad & Tobago	FranklinCovey West Indies	Tel: +868 652 6805	Email: lcg@rave-tt.net Web: www.fcla.com
Uruguay	FranklinCovey Uruguay	Tel: +59 8 2 628 6139	Email: franklincoveyur@fcla.com Web: www.fcla.com
Venezuela	FranklinCovey Venezuela	Tel: +58 212 2350468	Email: jmrconsultores@cantv.net
USA: Global head office	FranklinCovey Co	Tel: +1 801 975 1776	Email: comments@franklincovey.com Web: www.franklincovey.com

Asia Pacific

Australia	Franklin Covey Pty Ltd	Tel: +61 7 3259 0222	Email: info@franklincovey.com.au Web: www.franklincovey.com.au
India, Sri Lanka, Maldives, Bhutan, Nepal, Bangladesh	FranklinCovey South Asia	Tel: +91 124 5013032 +91 9811174447	Email: lavleen@franklincoveyindia.com Web: www.franklincoveysouthasia.com
Indonesia	FranklinCovey Indonesia Services	Tel: 65 021 572 0761	Email: info@dunamis.co.id Web: www.dunamis.co.id
Japan	FranklinCovey Japan	Tel: +81 3 3264 7417	Web: www.franklincovey.co.jp
Malaysia	Leadership Resources (Malaysia) Sdn. Bhd.	Tel: +603 79551148	Email: covey@po.jaring.my Web: www.franklincoveymalaysia.com
Philippines	Center for Leadership and Change, Inc.	Tel: +632 817 2726	Email: covey@clci.ph Web: www.clci.ph
Singapore & China	Centre for Effective Leadership (Asia) Pte Ltd.	Tel: +65 6838 0777	Email: training@cel-asia.com Web: www.highlyeffectiveleaders.com
South Korea	Korea Leadership Center	Tel: +82 2 2106 4100	Email: kengimm@eklc.co.kr Web: www.eklc.co.kr
Taiwan	Strategic Paradigm Consulting Co., Ltd.	Tel: +886 2 2657 8860	Email: smart@smartlearning.com.tw Web: www.smartlearning.com.tw
Thailand	PacRim Leadership Center Co., Ltd.	Tel: +66 2 728 1224 Fax: +66 2 728 0211	Email: plc@pacrimgroup.com Web: www.pacrimgroup.com

ABOUT THE AUTHOR

DR. STEPHEN R. COVEY is cofounder/vice chairman of FranklinCovey Company, a leading global professional services firm. FranklinCovey offers learning and performance solutions to assist professionals and organizations in significantly increasing their effectiveness in productivity, leadership, communications, and sales. Dr. Covey is perhaps best known as the author of *The 7 Habits of Highly Effective People,* which is ranked as a No. 1 best-seller by *The New York Times,* having sold more than thirteen million copies in thirty-six languages throughout the world. The book's message has created lasting impact, its sales keeping it on numerous best-seller lists for years. Dr. Covey is an internationally respected leadership authority, family expert, teacher, and organizational consultant. He has made teaching principle-centered living and principle-centered leadership his life's work.

- In 2002, *Forbes* named *The 7 Habits of Highly Effective People* one of the top ten most influential management books ever.
- A survey by *Chief Executive* magazine recognized *The 7 Habits of Highly Effective People* as one of the two most influential business books of the twentieth century. Dr. Covey also authored the book *Principle-Centered Leadership,* with sales exceeding one million copies.
- *The 7 Habits of Highly Effective People* audiobook on tape is the best-

selling nonfiction audiobook in history, selling more than 1.5 million copies.

- *First Things First,* coauthored by A. Roger and Rebecca R. Merrill, in its first year sold twice as many copies as did the hardcover edition of *The 7 Habits of Highly Effective People* in the same time period. More than two million copies have been sold. Simon & Schuster expressed the opinion, "*First Things First* is the best-selling time management book ever."
- Dr. Covey's *The 7 Habits of Highly Effective Families* was published in October 1997 and was ranked fourth on *The New York Times* best-seller list within three months. It is the number one best-selling hardcover book on the family. His newest books are *The Nature of Leadership,* co-authored with Roger Merrill and Dewitt Jones, and *Living the 7 Habits: Stories of Courage and Inspiration.*

Dr. Covey is the recipient of the Thomas More College Medallion for continuing service to humanity and has been awarded seven honorary doctorates. Other awards given Dr. Covey include the Sikhs' 1998 International Man of Peace Award, the 1994 International Entrepreneur of the Year Award, *Inc.* magazine's Services Entrepreneur of the Year Award, and, in 1996, the National Entrepreneur of the Year Lifetime Achievement Award for Entrepreneurial Leadership. He has also recently been recognized as one of *Time* magazine's twenty-five most influential Americans and one of *Sales and Marketing Management's* top twenty-five power brokers. Dr. Covey is currently serving on the board of directors for the Points of Light Foundation.

Dr. Covey earned his undergraduate degree from the University of Utah, his MBA from Harvard, and completed his doctorate at Brigham Young University. While at Brigham Young University, he served as assistant to the president and was also a professor of business management and organizational behavior.

Dr. Covey's organizational legacy to the world is Covey Leadership Center. On May 30, 1997, a merger with Franklin Quest created the new Franklin-Covey Company with more than three thousand employees and $350 million in annual revenue. Dr. Covey's vision of empowering organizations to implement principle-centered leadership in their cultures will continue to be an important focus of the FranklinCovey Company.

**SIMON &
SCHUSTER**

THE 8th HABIT

From Effectiveness to Greatness

Stephen R. Covey

In his multimillion-copy bestselling 7 Habits series,
Stephen Covey showed us how to become as effective
as it is possible to be. Now he takes the next step.
In *The 8th Habit* Covey urges us beyond effectiveness
towards true personal greatness. We all have the
potential to achieve this and we can do it by finding the
right balance of four human attributes: talent, need,
conscience and passion.

At the nexus of these attributes is what Covey calls
voice – the unique personal significance we each
possess. He exhorts us to move into the realm of
greatness and shows us how to do so, by engaging
our strengths and locating our powerful,
individual voices.

ISBN 0 7432 0682 7

£17.99

SIMON &
SCHUSTER

THE 7 HABITS OF HIGHLY EFFECTIVE PEOPLE

Stephen R. Covey

One of the world's bestselling, personal and professional development titles, with over 15 million copies sold, and now with new material to celebrate the 15th Anniversary!

Dr Covey reveals a simple but profoundly resonant pathway for living that encourages us to take full responsibility for our lives, and to live it with dignity, integrity and courage, transforming our performance, our effectiveness, the way we are viewed by the world and our self-respect.

ISBN 0 684 85839 8

£10.99

SIMON &
SCHUSTER

FIRST THINGS FIRST

Stephen R. Covey

Covey and A. Roger Merrill apply the insights of the
7 Habits to encourage us to develop a time-management
plan and to cope with the ever-increasing demands of
the workplace.

ISBN 0 684 85840 1

£10.99

PRINCIPLE-CENTRED LEADERSHIP

Stephen R. Covey

Covey invites you to centre your life and leadership
around principles such as fairness, equity, justice and
integrity that constitute the roots of every family and
institute that has ever prospered.

ISBN 0 684 85841 X

£10.99

**SIMON &
SCHUSTER**

This book and other **Simon & Schuster** titles are available from your local bookshop or can be ordered direct from the publisher.

Please send cheque or postal order for the value
of the book, **free postage and packing within
the UK**, to: SIMON & SCHUSTER CASH SALES
PO Box 29, Douglas, Isle of Man, IM99 1BQ
Tel: 01624 677237, Fax 01624 670923
bookshop@enterprise.net
www.bookpost.co.uk

Please allow 14 days for delivery. Prices and availability subject
to change without notice.